T0224282

Core-Task Design:

A Practice-Theory Approach to Human Factors

Synthesis Lectures on Human-Centered Informatics

Editor
John M. Carroll, *Penn State University*

Human-Centered Informatics (HCI) is the intersection of the cultural, the social, the cognitive, and the aesthetic with computing and information technology. It encompasses a huge range of issues, theories, technologies, designs, tools, environments, and human experiences in knowledge work, recreation and leisure activity, teaching and learning, and the potpourri of everyday life. The series publishes state-of-the-art syntheses, case studies, and tutorials in key areas. It shares the focus of leading international conferences in HCI.

Core-Task Design: A Practice-Theory Approach to Human Factors
Leena Norros, Paula Savioja, and Hanna Koskinen

ISBN: 978-3-031-01083-5 print
ISBN: 978-3-031-02211-1 ebook

DOI 10.1007/978-3-031-02211-1

A Publication in the Springer series
SYNTHESIS LECTURES ON HUMAN-CENTERED INFORMATICS #27
Series Editor: John M. Carroll, Penn State University

Series ISSN 1946-7680   Print 1946-7699 Electronic

Core-Task Design:

A Practice–Theory Approach to Human Factors

Leena Norros, Paula Savioja, and Hanna Koskinen
VIT Technical Research Centre of Finland, Ltd.

SYNTHESIS LECTURES ON HUMAN-CENTERED INFORMATICS #27

ABSTRACT

This book focuses on design of work from the human-factors (HF) perspective. In the approach referred to as Core-Task Design (CTD), work is considered practice, composed of human actors, the physical and social environment, and the tools used for reaching the actors' objectives. This book begins with consideration of an industrial case, the modernization of a nuclear power plant automation system, and the related human-system interfaces in the control room. This case illustrates generic design dilemmas that invite one to revisit human-factors research methodology: Human factors should adopt practice as a new unit of analysis and should accept intervention as an inherent feature of its methodology. These suggestions are put into practice in the CTD approach, according to which three general design functions are performed, those being:

- understand-to-generalize—empirical analysis of the work at hand,

- foresee-the-promise—creation of concepts for future work, and

- intervene-to-develop—participatory development and design of work.

For fulfillment of each of the design functions, several CTD methods are introduced. The methods are aimed at modeling the core task and analyzing how the actors actually take the core task features into account in order to achieve balance between potentially conflicting demands in action. Thereby, new understanding of the core task is acquired. Further methods focus on projecting the roles and functionality of technologies in the future work and on implementing changes to the work. Specific studies of the nuclear power plant's control-room renewal constitute an example demonstrating a core task and the associated methods. We argue that the CTD approach offers clear utility for the design of future technology, work, and everyday services and environments.

CTD utilizes achievements of practice theory in the social sciences to generate a creative synthesis of Cognitive Work Analysis, semiotic analysis of practice, and the cultural-historical theory of activity. Core-Task Design facilitates dialogue among human-factors experts, design engineers, and end users in their joint development of work. The intended audience of this book is students, researchers, and practitioners of human factors, industrial art and design, and instrumentation and control-system design.

KEYWORDS

human factors, practice theory, activity theory, cognitive work analysis, functional modeling, ecological approach, core task, habit, orientation, human-factors design, nuclear power plant, complex socio-technical systems, human–computer interaction

Contents

Acknowledgments

During the preparation of this book, we have had the pleasure of working with Prof. John M. Carroll, the knowledgeable visionary who is editor of the Synthesis Lectures on Human-Centered Informatics series. Also, we greatly appreciate the professional, friendly, and timely help that we always received from Morgan & Claypool Executive Editor Diane Cerra. In addition, we wish to express our gratitude for the review comments received from Prof. Bonnie Nardi, Prof. Viktor Kaptelinin, and Dr. Brian Kleiner, which helped us improve the manuscript. Errors and omissions in the final outcome remain our own. Warm thanks go also to Anna Shefl, who helped to clarify our message by correcting and improving the language of the manuscript.

Preface

Human-factors work is defined as a design discipline, but it has proved difficult to pay heed to this intrinsic element effectively in real-world design practice. While digital information technology and Internet-based communication create new possibilities for work and services in all spheres of life, they challenge people's learned ways of thinking, acting, and collaborating. Addressing these challenges effectively in design performed by human-factors professionals requires the discipline's methods and tools to develop, along with its ways of participating in the design processes. This book provides one perspective for analysis of digitalized work and everyday services and for improving our discipline's input to their design.

The approach described in this book has emerged in the course of several years of human-factors research at VTT Technical Research Center of Finland. The research environment of a multi-disciplinary research institute has promoted research giving input from several technical fields on customers' practice-relevant problems and has facilitated collaboration with customers representing a broad spectrum of domains.

The approach introduced here is characterized as a practice-theory approach to human factors. The claim defended in this work is that a practice-theory approach has potential to capture human activity in a context-dependent manner and appreciate the role of tools and technologies in human conduct. Hence, it has an intrinsic capability to develop good interplay with engineering and other relevant design-oriented disciplines.

There are three main arguments in support of the above claim. First, shifting the key concept and the unit of analysis in human-factors activities from the traditional "action" to "practice" means that the focus of research is redefined to encompass the totality of the socially distributed ways of acting instead of emphasize the individual and his or her mental processes. It follows from this that the design of technologies under such an approach is not human-centered in the usual sense. Instead, it is ecological, entailing emphasis on the mutual relationships of the environment, technology, and human actors. Focusing on the joint functioning of these main elements enables design of sustainable future technologies, services, and living environments.

The second argument is related to how practices are formed and perpetuated. A practice-theory-based approach acknowledges the power of cultural, social, and technological structures in shaping the content and forms of practices, but it also emphasizes and represents an interest in uncovering people's intentions, the meanings given to these structures, and the capability of people to develop practices and social and technological structures.

The final main argument has to do with the variety of theoretical conceptions of the notion of practice. This diversity becomes a strength for the concept through the possibility of identifying sufficient commonality among the various conceptions. In consequence, different perspectives can be brought together in a theoretically sound synthesis that fits the practical problems to be studied.

The authors believe that adoption of the concept of practice as the central methodological tool is novel within human-factors approaches. This does not mean that we would not acknowledge attempts representing similar reorientation, especially those in human–computer interaction research. In fact, joint interest in the practice-theory approach could be an important incentive for strengthening interaction between the human factors and human–computer interaction communities. Our approach shares with the systems-theory-oriented line of human-factors research the intention to view human behavior holistically. Reflecting on the connections between practice-theory- and socio-technical-system-based approaches would be fruitful.

The relatively restricted space for these lecture notes in the context of the Morgan & Claypool series led us to concentrate on describing the roots and characteristics specific to our approach, Core-Task Design methodology. We hope the future will offer opportunities to exploit the connections among relevant research approaches to create a comprehensive understanding of how human-factors theory and methodology can be developed further. We consider today's students and young researchers to play a central role in integrating approaches and developing practices for effective support of design related to technologically and societally complex work, everyday services, and living environments.

The authors of this book have collaborated intensively over several years in many research projects. The chance to prepare these lecture notes together gave us an opportunity to reflect on our previous work and to put the pieces of our methodology in place in a clear and consistent picture. This book has its broader background in the work of the human-factors research group at VTT Technical Research Center of Finland. In preparing this volume, the authors have had the opportunity to summarize and extensively exploit the achievements of this research group. We express tremendous gratitude to the other members of the group: Maaria Nuutinen, Jari Laarni, Leena Salo, Marja Liinasuo, Iina Aaltonen, Hannu Karvonen, and Mikael Wahlström.

CHAPTER 1

Introduction

Here, we present a new view of human factors and propose a coherent perspective for application in the study, development, and design of complex work systems. In so doing, we find that the methods developed to tackle today's highly complex work systems can be adopted even more widely in the design of future technologies, work, everyday services, and living environments. The research and design approach that we describe provides orientation towards solving practical problems in work and modern living in a conceptually solid manner that also affords creation of new scientific knowledge of human activity.

The human-factors (HF) discipline involves analysis, development, and design of work in close connection with engineering and domain expertise. The interest in work ties in with international human-factors and ergonomics tradition, but we also consider ourselves close to trends in the human–computer interaction (HCI) approach of studying man–machine interaction in context (e.g., computer-supported collaborative work). Furthermore, we find that ethnographically oriented workplace studies and—on account of their deep interest in work and activity in real-world situations—also Francophone ergonomics traditions are closely linked to our concept of human factors.

In the present discussion, we will draw on experience we gained in collaborating in design projects for technologically highly mediated and typically safety-critical work. Examples of such work are navigation of large ships, control of paper machines, anaesthetists' work in the operating theatre, and the nuclear power plant (NPP). In all of these contexts, our responsibility has been to understand how people in their normal work perceive the environment, make decisions, act, collaborate, or develop their competencies, alongside what demands the associated issues impose for the design of tools for professional users. The research accomplished in the NPP domain is examined in greater depth in this book in order to avoid placing the burden on the reader of shifting track between different work domains.

Those features of work that so far have characterized primarily large, safety-critical systems or processes are expected to become more generally typical of work and of everyday services and living environments. This is due to the global changes that influence modern societies, First, rapid change in the operating environment is evidenced by, for example, globalized business models, shifts in core market areas, and emergence of new enabling technologies. This means that distributed and Internet-based networked organizations will be the dominant form within which work is situated. The increasing availability of Internet-based services, such as healthcare or taxation services, will support various functions in a person's private life. The design of these services assumes end-user capability of exploiting the new tools and also their design from a holistic perspective.

Second, both the owners and providers of production and services and the customers require improved efficiency and product and service quality from these systems. Society also sets strict requirements for safety, health, and environmental protection. In regulated areas such as nuclear power production, this readily leads to tension between the needs of rapid innovation, on one hand, and the use of controlled design processes and traditional, proven solutions, on the other.

Third, the increasing complexity of socio-technical systems creates a major challenge not only for system developers but also for regulators and systems' operators/maintainers, extending even, in the case of various (typically Internet-based) services, to all members of the society. For example, the use of automation, remote services, and robotics is expected to increases greatly in industry, transportation, and the service sector in the near future. This prompts a key question: "What kinds of systems can be profitably and safely managed with the current technologies and human resources, and how could the complexity be minimized or better managed?"

The engineering solutions for meeting these challenges must encompass system development and continuous improvement ensuring certain capabilities. The traditional factors, such as low-cost, sufficient performance, and reliable implementation of the functions agreed upon at the outset, are not sufficient anymore. Today's socio-technical systems must be able to adapt themselves to situations that were not anticipated during the design stage. This adaptability could be manifested in dynamic function allocation: moving control between technology and the human in the course of operation of a system. These requirements may involve threats or new opportunities in the business environment and technology or might present unexpected phenomena and failures within the system itself. To cope with these situations, socio-technical systems must be resilient—i.e., intelligent in adapting and in combining their existing capabilities. An example of a resilient system per this definition is one in which the personnel have sufficient competence to determine an appropriate way of responding to a system failure that extends beyond the design assumptions of the system.

In development of design approaches for creating resilient systemic tools and environments in which people work side by side with the technology, it is more than reasonable to learn from the design experiences that have already been gained in the most challenging domains. The nuclear power plant is one of these. In recent years, we have been involved with automation and control-room renewal processes that have taken place in Finland's NPPs. Safety constraints in the design of the processes for renewal are very strict in this domain, and there is also insight to be considered with respect to the need for taking human factors into account. In the course of the extended collaboration with designers, we found it important to reflect on our role as human-factors experts and arrived at the conclusion that there is a need for methodological innovation.

The name "Core-Task Design" refers to the fact that within every activity it is possible to identify a "core": the generic key content that is relatively stable and unaffected by the current ways of accomplishing the activity, toward which core the activity should be oriented in order to be appropriate and develop. The core is the reason the activity exists; for instance, in nuclear power production, we may say that the core consists of electricity production, maintenance of safety, and economic efficiency. These exist in relation to phenomena regulated by the laws of nature, which cannot be altered via design interventions. While the core may seem obvious, the general purpose or mission of the activity may sometimes become blurred in the presence of elements such as overt organizational routines or clumsy and inappropriate tools. Understanding the core of the activity requires empirical scrutiny of that activity, and the core also changes as activities progress and develop. By naming the approach Core-Task Design (CTD), we aim to emphasize that human-factors work has a significant role in keeping the core task of the activity clear in the midst of projects of diverse types that are undertaken to improve some aspects of the activity.

1.1   MODERNIZATION OF THE NPP CONTROL ROOM

As do many other industrial processes, the nuclear power process proceeds mainly on its own, but it requires at the same time continuous human supervision and occasional control operations. For this purpose, the human operators are equipped with extensive and sophisticated instrumentation and control (I&C) systems (i.e., the automation system). Some of the equipment for monitoring and control is situated at distributed control points on the shop floor, but most is in the main control room, in which the 24/7 monitoring and control work takes place. Traditionally, the control rooms are large spaces with hard-wired control panels on all of the walls providing information on the process via various types of instruments. Levers and buttons are available for steering the process. Further information and control possibilities are provided from the control desks, arranged in a layout that allows the operators a broad but in-depth view of the control room and fellow operators' activities, along with, indirectly, the remote process.

A control-room operating team at a Finnish NPP is composed of three persons. Two operators supervise and control designated parts of the process in accordance with the work regimen, and the team is led by the shift supervisor. The team as a unit is prepared to manage the process in all its states—i.e., in normal operations, in planned transitions of production, and in cases of disturbance and accident—and the operators are also prepared and equipped to handle serious accidents. All work is supported by operating procedures of various kinds, and the work assumes close communication and collaboration both within the operator team and with other personnel. Field operators, stationed on the shop floor, frequently visit the control room to coordinate their tasks with the ongoing control-room work. During maintenance or testing periods, the control room serves as a command and coordination center for all operations in the process and dozens of people may remain in the control room or visit it.

High reliability of the automated system, coupled with competent monitoring and control activities performed by the human operators, is clearly a significant prerequisite for the safety of an NPP. The desired reliability of the collaborative human–technology system performance is reached via detailed and extensive safety measures and through continuous efforts to diminish uncertainty in the system. All changes to the system are made with great care, and they are always preceded by comprehensive analysis of the proposed changes' impact on the overall safety of the system. The safety principles applied for ensuring the reliability and safety of the automated systems are tailored to identify vulnerabilities that are typical of hard-wired analog instrumentation technology. New types of problems emerge when automation is based on programmable digital technology. It is easy to understand that there is well-motivated reluctance to embrace technological innovations in such a situation. The overall mindset is oriented to remaining with solutions that have been proved to work reliably.

Nonetheless, the digital turn in the path of the technological basis of modern society has not left nuclear power plants untouched. Digital user interface technology made its way to plants' main control rooms several decades ago. Typically, digital technology was long ago implemented in the process-monitoring systems that analyze and present process data to be used by control-room operators. Much more comprehensive changes, covering also the actions controlling the process, are now being designed and implemented as the automation and the control-room systems age. Upgrades are motivated mainly by the obsolescence of the analog technology in use and the difficulty of finding spare parts. A positive incentive is that the new digital technology offers great advantages with regard to the computation, management, and presentation of process information, technology that should make the control and monitoring more efficient. Yet there remains a great challenge in the design: demonstrating the digital systems' reliability and safety.

Digital Desktop Based

Conventional Analog

Smart Ubiquitous

Figure 1.1: An illustration of the evolution of control-room work as a function of the possibilities of automation and interface technology.

Figure 1.1 illustrates the shift in the technological foundations of NPP process control. Our focus is on how the shift from predominantly analog to predominantly digital technology manifests itself in the control room concepts (in the first transition in Figure 1.1). In the shift to the digital-desktop-based phase, further possibilities offered by "smart" and ubiquitous I&C technology with an Internet connection, especially for the retrieval and presentation of information, are in sight already (this is the second transition in Figure 1.1). This potential of technology imposes pressure to implement solutions that already are available in other industrial environments.

1.2 HUMAN-FACTORS CHALLENGES IN THE CONTROL-ROOM DESIGN CASE

The design of the automation renewal in this context is a complex matter, and the strict safety requirements make it even more difficult. Why then complicate things more by imposing additional demands related to human factors? Cannot human-factors issues be resolved later in the design process? We are fortunate that such reasoning is considered outdated and inappropriate. Today, human-factors work constitutes its own track in the design process. Still, contributing usefully to the design is a challenge for human-factors experts. Some of the general problems that we encountered in our example case are presented below.[1]

1.2.1 AMBIGUITY ABOUT WHAT MAKES A GOOD CONTROL ROOM

The control room is the nerve center of the nuclear power plant. Huge amounts of incoming information from the process and a wide variety of control equipment that can influence the process are concentrated within one big room. Here, everything has to form an ordered whole so that it is possible to make sense of the process situation, understand the availability of control resources, make decisions in a manner ensuring appropriate operations, and implement the actions implied, all this in good coordination with one's fellow operators. As NPP operations is a safety-critical field, it is crucial to predict what changes are to be expected in the operators' work in connection with the digitalization of the automation and control-room systems.

Some excellent studies, such as those of O'Hara et al. (2003) and of Roth and O'Hara (2002), provide an overview of changes that digital technologies can be expected to bring. These studies are well known and widely cited. Important contributions to the nuclear field's human-factors research methodology have been developed at the human-factors research facility HAMMLAB within the OECD Halden Reactor Project (Skjerve and Bye, 2011; Skraaning Jr. et al., 2007). However, results of many international HAMMLAB studies, alongside other studies, paint quite an ambiguous picture of the impacts of digitalization. Operators may, for instance, feel that desktop-based interfaces enable better management and control of the production process on account of the greater quantities of information, but, because of the small viewing area of the computer screens, the overview of the process state might be endangered (Huang and Hwang, 2009; Laarni et al., 2006). The studies

---

[1]   The careful reader may notice that the challenges are quite generic to any technological development in which expertise in the human sciences is required in addition to skills in traditional engineering fields.

also show that operators' opinions differ as to the extent to which digital human–system interfaces affect collaboration, cooperation, and communication between operators. Further ambiguity exists with regard to the mental load associated with various control-room concepts. One can readily be overwhelmed by the sheer quantity of data available in a digitalized control room; this renders it difficult to find the relevant information (Kaarstad et al., 2011; O'Hara and Persensky, 2011), but the opinion is also expressed that digitalized user interfaces diminish the mental load entailed by searching for information (Savioja et al., 2012b; Yang et al., 2010).

When one is enquiring about what qualifies a tool as a good one, it would be natural to consult relevant standards. The main guidelines used for NPP control rooms' design are found in NUREG-0700 (NUREG0700, 2002), now being updated, on review of the interface design. It was established before the digital era, and even the update under preparation will not cover issues specific to digitalized control rooms. More up-to-date support for design is provided by ISO 11640 (NUREG0700, 2002)and several field-specific ISO standards. These are found useful also for NPP control-room design (Automation, 2010).

The key issue, however, is that, while standards and guidelines offer good, detailed advice for user-interface design, they lack an explicit conceptual basis and generic insight into what constitutes the target state, the good control room for which to strive (Norros and Savioja, 2004). The same problem hinders interpretation of research results. It is not explicit which control-room design features result in or support good operating practice. Therefore, guidance for design of digital control-room systems is insufficient or utterly lacking. Good quality in a control room could perhaps be defined through identification of the generic roles that the control room should fulfill in work practice, as authors such as Hannu Paunonen (1997) have proposed. In conjunction with this, it would also be possible to identify how specific interface solutions contribute to the tool functions striven for.

1.2.2   LACK OF INSIGHT INTO GOOD OPERATOR WORK

In itself, the variation in research results to do with operator performance or in operators' opinions about the technologies is not surprising. It is difficult for human-factors experts and for the end users too to comprehend the tools in their future use. One is caught in the dilemma that the requirements of the new tools get comprehended within the frame of the tasks of the present work, which is not a sufficient basis from which to design or evaluate future tools, because the designed technology itself changes the task demands and the requirements thereby imposed for the tools. This phenomenon, identified some time ago, has been labeled the "task–artifact cycle" (Carroll et al., 1991). It appears to be a fundamental dilemma in the design of tools and difficult to overcome.

If the quality of tools is measured in terms of their operators' performance, how performance is measured is, of course, decisive for the validity of the results. In the long history of human-factors research, it has become customary to measure task achievement by means of performance-outcome-related measurements (e.g., time for task fulfillment or error rate) or cognitively related outcome measures, such as situation awareness or the mental load involved in the task. The background for the metrics lies in the information-processing steps behind individual human actions. These measurements are suitable in comparison of test results achieved under disparate conditions or while different tools are in use. They do not yield direct insight into how individual features of the tools shaped the ways of acting or into the intentions behind the actions. Therefore, use of performance-outcome metrics should be complemented by measurements that reveal how the features of the tools support or hinder work. The challenge then is to develop a vocabulary for specification of characteristics of ways or modes of acting that could be argued to facilitate appropriate or less appropriate acting. Appropriateness expresses the potential of the professional actions in question to bring good outcomes in various circumstances, though it is not necessarily always reflected in the outcome of a specific task performance. Professional actors typically reach a good performance outcome also in less favourable circumstances. The tools of the work have a central role in supporting the potential for such good action. Developing criteria and metrics for use in identifying the appropriateness of action chains assumes that human-factors experts inform themselves of what the relevant professional user community values as good work and a solid professional ethos. Studying tools and their use as a unit should also be required, so that their mutual impact on the quality of acting can be captured. This necessitates scrutiny of the generic functions of tools in the real activity contexts and analysis of how the tools actually are used. Neither value-based considerations of appropriate acting nor general insight into human–technology joint system functions can be determined by human-factors research that describes acting via performance-outcome measures alone.

1.2.3   DESIGN PRODUCTS AS UNIQUE ENTITIES

The exploitation of human-factors knowledge in control-room design faces a fundamental challenge arising from the fact that each control room is a unique case. The way information is expressed in the user interface is tailored to the case, and, for security and safety reasons, sharing very detailed information on the solutions is not even allowed. It appears, furthermore, that, by nature, digital technology allows greater variety of design solutions than is typical for analog technology; this results in even greater uniqueness of each control room. Therefore, it is hard to acquire or develop information that would be valid for control rooms in general. This is also one reason for the ambiguity of results of control rooms' evaluation, discussed above.

This uniqueness adds a further challenge to finding a reference for their evaluation. An important requirement that emerges from the particularity of the product is that "good" must be defined at a higher level of abstraction, thereby leaving room for fulfilling the demands specific to each case.

1.2.4   THE MARRIAGE OF USABILITY AND SAFETY

The architecture of digital automation at an NPP is based on the so-called defence-in-depth principle, according to which the entire system needs to include a set of technical or organizational barriers to prevent chains of more severe consequences of plant failure. In the process of considering the digitalization of the automation system, typical failure modes and vulnerabilities of program-based I&C systems are taken into account, and several safety-design principles—e.g., those of redundancy, diversity, and separation—are followed for creation of such defences. Human operators are seen as the final defence. However, because safety is typically considered to entail non-existence of failure and human error is deemed to be the main source of failure, the conclusion is that human intervention in the process should, by and large, be reduced. Less prevalent is the idea that human actors, in combination with appropriate technology, create capabilities for safety through anticipation, adaptation, and learning (Hollnagel, 2006). Hence, optimizing the joint operation of the technical system and the operators in view of human-factors-based usability criteria is not considered the primary issue with regard to safety.

Our conclusion is that human-factors work should support attempts to expand the concept of safety to encompass the adaptive potential of human actors to create capacity for safety. It should facilitate development of the concept of tools' usability such that the separation between safety and usability as targets of good design disappears. In situations wherein safety demands appear to compromise good usability, the human-factors discipline should support analysis of the causes of the conflict and contribute to reconsideration of the underlying concept in the human–technology coupling's operation (Amalberti, 2006).

1.2.5   CONSIDERING TRAINING AS DESIGN

Earlier, when digitalization of control rooms focused on the process-information systems and the consequences of digitalization for the work were restricted to monitoring of the process, the related operator training emphasized primarily familiarizing the operators with handling the new equipment. It was accepted as sufficient that the operators appropriate the tools, incorporating them into their work practices spontaneously, by experience. The present changes in the automation and the control-room environment are more profound, especially because they also affect control operations, among them safety-classified operations. In this situation, the operative organization and the designers begin to agree that the operators must be involved proactively in the change of technology, with one possibility being systematic participation of the operators, as end users, in the design process. This option was effectively exploited in one of the cases we studied, in which the in-house design department took a central role in the design of the control room.

Operators' participation in design does not respond fully to all the training needs. It is evident that operator training must be much more comprehensive, but the most important element is that it must consider the possibility that the technology itself may require changes and that changes in roles, responsibilities, and the content of the operators' tasks are to be anticipated. It has also emerged that the existing understanding as to what kind(s) of conceptual knowledge operators would need in order to understand the principles of digital automation and its consequences for both plant safety and their own operative behavior is insufficient. Also required is better insight into how to combine instruction pertaining to the features of the tools, teaching of operation skills, conveying of conceptual knowledge of process phenomena, etc. (Laarni et al., 2011). All of these needs may be discovered in the course of the training.

1.2.6 THE ROLE OF EVALUATION IN DESIGN

Understanding the deep hierarchical structure of the complex control-room system and identifying how to exploit human-factors knowledge to best effect in its design process are very difficult. But it is also challenging to grasp how the changes in the technology transform the entire concept of operations that provides a framework for the division of tasks and responsibilities between the operators and the technical control system. Not all of the questions raised can be answered ahead of time, but they do need to be dealt with during design. On-line evaluation of the design outputs is necessary throughout the process—this evaluation is an inherent part of the design. Human factors are central here: the evaluation involves mainly testing the tools in use. The control-room design projects in which we were involved revealed that the authoritative international standard for human-factors review of nuclear power plant control rooms (NUREG0711, 2004) did not provide sufficient support for on-line monitoring of the highly complex and step-wise design necessary so would need adaptation and fleshing out. Integration of the accumulating test results is a particular challenge, as is the dilemma of how one can remain independent with regard to design while still delivering relevant feedback for use in the design.

1.3 METHODOLOGICAL CONSEQUENCES

The challenges we faced when striving to provide human-factors support in the design of NPP control rooms exemplify general problems of addressing human factors in design, and, indeed, we have encountered them in our design-oriented studies in other industrial domains (e.g., the maritime industry, manufacturing, and smart Internet-supported farming). Other scientists and practitioners have made corresponding observations. Recently, the role of human factors in design was discussed in the main international human-factors forums (Dul et al., 2012; Wilson and Carayon, 2014), along with HCI forums (Kuutti and Bannon, 2014). There appears to be widespread agreement that a more systemic or holistic approach to human behavior as a foundation for human factors or HCI research would be fruitful. In fact, there are established research approaches in work studies that speak to this gap. While they currently have only a small role on the human-factors research agenda, they could contribute more to the progress sought in the human-factors discipline. The potential of these influences will be discussed further in the next chapter.

Even though there might be a number of human-factors-external reasons for today's overly modest exploitation of human-factors knowledge in design, as shown by, for instance, Jan Dul et al. (2012), we feel that it is necessary to begin changing the situation by addressing issues at the core of the discipline (Norros, 2014). Progress with regard to these would have an influence on the use of human-factors knowledge generally. The conclusion we can draw from our experience is that there is a need to develop the human-factors research methodology in two respects: First, the unit of analysis in human-factors works needs to be redefined, and, secondly, human-factors practitioners should adopt a developmental research approach. In consequence of these pressures on the methodology, new concepts explaining human conduct within the human-factors discipline have become relevant. These tendencies have shaped the Core-Task Design approach and served as reasons for the enrichment of CTD through a number of concepts that have not been widely used in today's human-factors research.

1.3.1   REDEFINING THE UNIT OF ANALYSIS

The first methodological elaboration we consider necessary has to do with redefining the unit of analysis with respect to design-oriented human factors. As our examples from NPP control-room design highlighted, current human-factors research focuses too much on individual information-processing aspects or elements of action. These are studied as dependent variables subject to various features of the environment or tools. We could label this orientation an (inter)action perspective in human-factors research. This very positivistic view of human behavior brings with it difficulties in integrating diverse results pertaining to the impact of technological change, in managing multiple goals (usability and safety in the NPP case), and in understanding of human reliability and safety. This view also neglects the fact that humans and technology form an entity that develops as a whole and that this joint functioning should be evaluated from a broader, technology-in-use perspective.

The above reasoning has led us to the conclusion that the unit for analysis of human factors should be redefined such that the relevant human conduct is comprehended as intentional patterned interplay of the subject, artifacts, and possibilities of the social and material environment. The possibilities of the environment are central for the meaning of this interplay. The appropriate unit of analysis is **practice**, and the complementary orientation in human-factors work is, accordingly, a **practice perspective**.

In this article, we take practice as a conceptual rather than an empirical category, in the spirit of Davide Nicolini (2013), who says that "adopting real-time practice as the starting point of social and organizational inquiry poses a specific challenge exactly because of what makes it interesting;

that is the fact that it constitutes the unsung background amid which we conduct our existence" (p. 217). Practice must be articulated in terms of further concepts and operationalized in empirical studies, and this process may—and should—be carried out in several ways. Hence, the concept of practice draws together a number of related concepts and approaches in the social and human sciences. In our case, the specific examples from the practice-theory family that we draw from are the cultural-historical theory of activity (CHAT) (Leont'ev, 1978; Vygotsky, 1978), the semiotic model of activity (Peirce, 1998a), and ecological-psychology-inspired work-domain analysis that is part of the Cognitive Work Analysis approach (Rasmussen, 1986; Vicente, 1999).

Practice refers to arrays of activity that emerge in the interplay of the actors with the environment. Accordingly, it cannot be directly designed. Taking the central concept of *activity system* from CHAT work, we can use it as an operationalization of practice for comprehension of the work system as a social entity. However, because our studies are focused on the design of work and tools, we have developed the concept of the *core task*, with the aid of which we get closer to the process of the mutual determination by organism and environment. The concept specifies the object of activity from the standpoint of what it takes to act upon it. The core task *delineates the generic developing content of the work and expresses itself as joint functions emerging from the meeting of the human organism's resources with the possibilities and constraints of the environment for reaching certain global objectives of work activity.* The core task is taken as a design object because the intrinsic human resources, the environmental possibilities and constraints, and the global objectives can be shaped by, for example, technologies.

Further categories in empirical analysis of practice are *activity*, *orientation*, *habit*, and *user experience*. We expand on these later. We propose that, in connection with the design for the core task, a generic definition addressing what constitutes a good tool needs to be developed. For this, we have developed the concept of *systems usability* (SU) for consideration of the goodness and the core-task-orientation of a technology concept.

1.3.2   ADOPTING A DEVELOPMENTAL RESEARCH APPROACH

The second methodological elaboration is to adopt a developmental research approach. This necessary transformation in the methodology is linked to the epistemic nature of the human-factors discipline. The discipline draws on the traditional concept of scientific knowledge, according to which knowledge is achieved in well-defined and controlled conditions with minimal influence by the researcher on the object of analysis. This concept, under which knowledge also is isolated from value judgements, does not really square with the circumstances in which human activity takes place and in which human-factors knowledge should be applied. Our NPP control-room case demonstrates this discrepancy between the scientific ideal of knowledge and the actual circumstances of exploiting human factors. It was found, for example, that integrating the diverse body of information about the work and technology requires comprehension of what is considered worth striving for, and what is held to be good work (i.e., the target values) must be considered in the design decisions. It was also found that the focus in design is on a unique object. If one wishes to have a reference for evaluating how the design is proceeding or to create generalizable knowledge for utilization in a further design context, it is necessary that the design target be handled on a higher level of abstraction. Functional modeling of work (Vicente, 1999) is found useful here, and we also propose extending the generic models with **functional situation models** that specify the circumstances in certain situations. A modeling approach known as **tools-in-use modeling** and an evaluation approach known as the **systems-usability case** draw on the concept of *systems usability*. The usability case approach was constructed to support design and evaluation that could extend the usual product design toward more generic results.

Finally, our control-room design example highlighted also that, in action upon the design object, knowledge of the object is achieved. The course of design can be steered on the basis of this more in-depth knowledge. **Formative intervention** is a means of changing the object and simultaneously creating new knowledge of the object, as is made evident in, for instance, developmental work research, a stream of CHAT (Engeström, 1987). The conceptual apparatus created for CTD enables maintaining sufficient objectivity while one intervenes in the design. The epistemology of CTD is developmental in nature.

The novelty of the Core-Task Design approach lies in use of the practice-theory perspective to form a creative synthesis of Cognitive Work Analysis, semiotic analysis of practice, and the cultural-historical theory of activity. We consider the synthesis sound because the approaches that it draws together share a common methodological base with roots in the practice-theory approach. Within this overall framework, we have created several concepts and methods with which complex work can be designed and developed.

1.3.3   SUMMARY OF THE METHODOLOGICAL CONSEQUENCES

A summary of the methodological consequences that tackling the design challenges of complex work creates with respect to human factors is provided in Table 1.1, below. We label our methodology a practice perspective on human factors, and we have proposed several new concepts that operationalize this practice perspective and enable empirical study of human conduct to support design aims. The concepts named in the table are explained in detail in the following chapters.

Table 1.1: Moving toward a practice perspective in human-factors activities: identified pressures for changing human factors research methodology (first column) by redefining the unit of analysis (second column) and by adopting a developmental research approach (third column), where the consequences of methodological change become evident in the new concepts and methods adopted in Core-Task Design (the concepts and methods are italicized)

Human-Factors Challenge	Redefining the Unit of Analysis	Adopting a Developmental Research Approach
1. Ambiguity as to what constitutes a good control room	Designing appropriate functionality of the tools requires methodical capability to consider user–tool interaction in specific situations in relation to generic features and objectives of the context or domain that provides the meaning of the interaction CTD concepts: *Activity, systems usability, tools-in-use modeling*	Both standards and current research lack an explicit conceptual foundation for the evaluation of tools that could be used as a reference for design. Design activity can gain from conceptually elaborated research on human factors CTD concepts: *Systems usability, tools-in-use modeling*
2. Lack of insight into the nature of good operator work	Generic-level reference for good action in certain work is required when one evaluates activity. Expression of appropriate focus in the object of work is involved CTD concept: *Core task* Tools and their use form a unit, which changes as a whole. Comprehensive expression of the use of tools is required for an understanding of practice CTD concepts: *Activity, orientation, habit, systems usability*	Generic-level definition of good acting in a certain work context could be used as a guide for design CTD concept: *Core task expressing the value toward which to steer design and training*
3. Each design product being unique	The uniqueness of each end product (e.g., control room) requires that the creative potential of professional users of the particular work be exploited effectively in the design CTD concept: *Formative interventions*	The definition of "good" must be at a higher level of abstraction, leaving room for meeting case-specific needs CTD concepts: *Functional modeling of the work, functional situation modeling, tools-in-use modeling, formative interventions*
4. Combining of usability and safety	For greater safety, the concept of safety must be expanded to cover human actors' adaptation potential CTD concept: *Systems usability*	If safety demands a compromise on good usability, human factors supports analysis of the causes of the conflict and contributes to reconsidering the basic human–technology concept of operations and the reference for good acting CTD concepts: *Core task, tools-in-use modeling*

5. Considering training as design	Solutions of digital technology become tools only via appropriation of the practices of their use CTD concepts: *Activity, systems usability*	Solutions of digital technology emerge when operators test the solutions in training CTD concept: *Formative interventions*
6. The role of evaluation in design	Evaluating a joint human–technology system solution requires diverse views of the performance of the professional users CTD concept: *Systems usability*	Evaluation results accumulated from several successive tests during the design must be integrated. Conceptual tools at a higher level of abstraction are necessary. Such a reference is needed also for maintaining independence and to support generalization from results CTD concepts: *Core task, systems usability, usability case*

1.4   THE STRUCTURE OF THE BOOK

The discussion continues with Chapter 2's introduction of the Core-Task Design methodology as a proposal for practice-oriented research into human factors. The main contribution is in the argument for the redefinition of the unit of analysis and derivation of a design model with three main functions: **understand-to-generalize**, **foresee-the-promise**, and **intervene-to-develop**. The design model responds to the need for a developmental methodology. We will make explicit those lines of research that we have borrowed to support CTD methodology. To fulfill each of the design functions, several novel modeling and analytical methods were developed. Arguments will be laid out for these methods, which Chapter 2 describes briefly.

The CTD methods are introduced in more detail in Chapters 3, 4, and 5. Each of these chapters focuses on one of the three design functions. Relevant empirical studies will be used as a vehicle of description of the CTD design function and the CTD methods. The studies are all from one domain, the NPP domain, which we hope makes it easier for the reader to grasp the conceptually rich methods. Chapter 3 describes the design function called understand-to-generalize, which is exemplified by empirically answering the question of how to generalize from empirical enquiry about actual work. Chapter 4 focuses on the foresee-the-promise design function, exemplified by empirically addressing how to see the promise of solutions for future work. Finally, Chapter 5 considers the function termed intervene-to-develop. In this connection, we shall give empirically grounded answers to the question of how to change the work system in practice.

Chapter 6 concludes the presentation of the Core-Task Design approach. First, we summarize the contributions of the approach. Then, the approach is situated against the broader backdrop of the global changes expected in work and the demands they impose for future design activities. Finally, the potential of the approach for tackling the ensuing design demands is reflected upon.

CHAPTER 2

Core-Task Design Methodology

On the basis of our experiences from the studies involving NPP control-room design, we have argued that, if human-factors research is to have more effect in the design of complex systems, the field's research methodology must be expanded. The two developments we proposed are redefinition of the unit of analysis and the adoption of a developmental research approach. Both changes are facilitated by application of the practice-theory perspective to human factors. Such a change in the research methodology creates pressure for renewal of the conceptual apparatus used in the empirical analyzes. In this chapter, we introduce our conceptual solutions proceeding from the two above-mentioned methodological developments.

At first glance, interest in the concept of practice does not seem to be very original. It appears, in fact, that the concept has been spontaneously adopted by human-factors experts who accomplish their research in the workplaces and develop practical solutions to problems in work and in organizations. It turns out that only a few of these experts have had the opportunity to occupy themselves with theoretical discussion of the basic concept they exploit in explaining human conduct or interest in this discussion. At the same time, the "practice turn"—that is, the general methodological shift and the theoretical discussion it has caused in the social and human sciences—may have gone unnoticed by the human-factors community. In consequence, "practice" is used as an intuitively appropriate and a fashionable idiom that replaces others—e.g., "action," "decision-making," "problem-solving," "performance," and "interaction."[2]

The practice paradigm has existed as an undercurrent in human–computer interaction research (Kuutti and Bannon, 2014). The cited authors give a concise but informative account of the history of the HCI and computer-supported co-operative work approach and identify two theoretical streams of HCI research that they consider complementary, the interaction paradigm and the practice paradigm. While the practice turn in the social sciences has been an openly partisan and reflective movement intended to create a new research focus, in the HCI field it has been tacit, spontaneous, and unsystematic, without any articulated program or indeed a clear recognition of this orientation to practice (Kuutti and Bannon, 2014, p. 3544). Consequently, the interaction paradigm has remained in a dominant role, forming the main stream of HCI research.

This is not the place for an account of the history of the influence of practice theory in human-factors research. Instead, we will propose one practice-oriented research approach and

---

[2] As an exception, the Francophone ergonomics tradition has a conceptual connection to the practice approach, via its adherence to the concept of activity, or activité. This concept has long had a central role and is widely adopted as the unit of analysis in this tradition (Daniellou, 2005; Daniellou and Rabardel, 2005).

demonstrate connections to the concept of practice employed. In doing so, we also provide answers to the questions that become apparent in relation to what would be gained via adoption of practice as a core category of focus among human factors.

2.1   THE PRACTICE APPROACH IN CORE-TASK DESIGN

To have a good starting point, one must be aware of the broad scope of the practice approach. Theodore Schatzki, one of the most prominent theoreticians in the practice-theory domain, writes that a practice-based approach makes decisive contributions to contemporary understanding of diverse issues, among them the philosophical and social-scientific significance of human activity; the nature of subjectivity, embodiment, rationality, meaning, and normativity; the character of language, science, and power; and the organization, reproduction, and transformation of social life. Consequently, the approach is multidisciplinary and the definitions of practice vary accordingly. It is necessary, therefore, to specify the scope of our interests and the definition we consider adequate for our research aims.

2.1.1   VARIETY AMONG THEORIES OF PRACTICE

Nicolini (2013) made a comprehensive attempt at a taxonomy characterizing the diversity in theories of practice. In his attempts to clarify the central message of this approach, one means is to identify six main streams of the general practice-theory approach. These range from the **praxeology** of Pierre Bourdieu and Anthony Giddens through **practice as tradition and community**, as represented by, for instance, Gene Lave and Etienne Wenger; **practice as activity**, represented by the cultural-historical theory of activity, especially with Yrjö Engeström; **practice as accomplishment**, represented by ethno-methodologists, especially Harold Garfinkel, or Harvey Sacks, Michael Lynch, and Lucy Suchman; and **practice as the house of the social**, in which aspect the thinking of Martin Heidegger and Ludwig Wittgenstein is developed most explicitly, chiefly by Schatzki, to, finally, **discourse as practice**, portrayed particularly in conversation analysis (e.g., by John Heritage) or, in a different way, in the discourse-analysis approach of Michel Foucault.

Of these streams of practice theory, we draw from that examining cultural-historically tuned practice as activity, the ethno-methodology-tuned stream that views practice as accomplishment, and the stream drawing on phenomenology and taking practice as the house of the social. We base our approach, in addition to the streams identified by Nicolini, on the philosophical tradition of American pragmatism, which emphasizes the ontological and epistemic role of practice. As will be shown later, our methodology exploits the work of pragmatists Charles Sanders Peirce and John Dewey for the development of tools for empirical analysis of practices.

One further practice-theory-relevant approach that was found important for our methodology is the ecological organism–environment joint-system approach. Without neglecting the social aspects of human conduct, this approach theorizes on the biological bases of human conduct. It focuses on the functional units that the organism and environment form together in human conduct (Gibson, 1979; Järvilehto, 1998; von Uexküll and Kriszat, 1932). The approach has close connection to the philosophical ideas of Maurice Merleau-Ponty (1986). We see that pragmatists' and ecological organism–environment joint-system approaches not only fit well in but also contribute significantly to the practice-theory framework, and we consider their application in our methodology theoretically acceptable.

2.1.2   THE DEFINITION OF PRACTICE USED IN CORE-TASK DESIGN

Schatzki provides a definition of the practice approach that would satisfy most practice theoreticians. Under his definition, the approach entails advocacy of a social ontology, which distances it from approaches that privilege individuals, (inter)actions, language, signifying systems, the life world, institutions/roles, structures, or systems in definition of the social. Schatzki's definition of practice is the following: "*Practices are embodied, materially mediated arrays of human activity centrally organized around shared practical understanding,*" which can only be analyzed via the field of practices (Schatzki et al. 2001, p. 11; see also Schatzki, 2005, p. 47 and Nicolini, 2013, pp. 164–167).

We adopt the above definition of practice. For demonstrating the gains that the practice-theory approach brings to the study of human behavior, we draw on the five characteristics that Nicolini (2013, pp. 3-6) cites as shared by practice theories. These are inserted in Table 2.1 in the left column. Proceeding from these five features, we articulate in the right column of the table the added value that each of these characteristics provides specifically for human-factors research into complex work.

Table 2.1: Shared characteristics of practice theories according to Nicolini (2013) (left column) and the added value that each characteristic would bring to human-factors research (right column)	
Shared characteristics of practice theories	**Added value to human-factors research**
Practice creates and perpetuates all aspects of social life via recursive two-way work between practice and its material conditions (or structure and process)	A practice approach provides background for understanding the interplay of organizational structures and the local and situated role of the sharp-end actors—e.g., in explaining phenomena such as safety culture in situated actions
Practice demonstrates the critical role of the human body and material things in all social affairs	A practice-oriented approach provides the foundation for a sound interdisciplinary approach to design of technologies as joint human–technology–environment systems

Practice is sense-making against a more or less stable background of other practices that draws on individuals' agency; focusing on practice is different from focusing on individual-level action	A practice-oriented approach confers freedom from the fruitless duality between technology push and human centered design by focusing on the usage of tools—i.e., technology in practice
Practice is not contrasted against knowledge; knowing is human conduct in which use of artifacts and discourse are decisive	A practice approach enables understanding of learning in work and the development of work, and it facilitates development of formative research and design methodologies
Practice takes into account that interests and power are central forces in all human behavior	The practice approach provides arguments for explicit consideration of values in the analysis of organizational culture and work activity and in the design of work

2.1.3   PRACTICE-BASED THEORIES AS A TOOLKIT FOR EMPIRICAL RESEARCH

Nicolini considers practice-oriented approaches to be tools for empirical research. He proposes that multiple practice theories could be used as a joint resource, a toolkit, for understanding the specific aspects of practice that are relevant in light of the focus and aims of the study. The validity of integrating several of the theories is grounded in the idea that these theories exhibit a number of "family resemblances"—i.e., that they form a network of overlapping similarities that allows considering them related (Nicolini, 2013, Chapter 9).

The methodological conclusion of Nicolini is well suited to our purpose of tackling the practical problems in human conduct that are of theoretical interest. Adopting the concept of practice has implications with regard to the vocabulary and methods associated with human conduct. An earlier work (Norros, 2004) was our first attempt in this direction. In that book, we proposed the use of the practice concept and introduced the Core-Task Analysis approach for the study of complex work. At that time, the possibility of connecting the developing approach to a distinct practice-theory perspective had not yet been identified. Instead, the approach was labeled ecological. Through this characterisation, we emphasized activity as an entity that emerges in mutual determination by the human and the social and physical environment. We sought a unit of analysis with which these elements would not be separate and through which one could focus on their joint functioning. This orientation is still valid. However, as our concrete research tasks have become more and more connected to design, it has been necessary to develop an understanding of the role of human factors from the design perspective. We have drawn especially from those streams of practice theory that are concerned with the development of practices. Most prominent in this respect is the "practice as activity" stream represented by CHAT. The cultural-historical theory of activity has great merits in considering how practices change the world and how they expand. The aim of the approach is to facilitate actors' development and organizations' change (Nicolini, 2013, pp. 105, 107). The shift in the labelling of our research approach from Core-Task Analysis to Core-Task Design reflects the change of focus in our research.

In the following discussion, we introduce the central concepts and methods of Core-Task Design. The presentation is organized such that we demonstrate how the concepts and methods of CTD tie in with the two main methodological aims: redefining the unit of analysis and of making the research methodology developmental in nature.

2.2   CONCRETIZING PRACTICE AS THE NEW UNIT OF ANALYSIS

In traditional human-factors work, the focus is on the phenomena of action and interaction. These are observed and tested through application of concepts and measurements that draw attention to the internal structure of cognitive or emotional events in finely specified tasks, often in strictly controlled conditions. With the practice approach, the focus shifts to observation and experimentation that examine how and according to what logic the actors and the environment, including tools, get organized into arrays of action with regard to the purposes of the work. These organized arrays of action express and are explained by their meaning. Thereby, practices exhibit rationales and the value of the situation or environment for people.

2.2.1   CONCEPTUAL DISTINCTIONS TO BE OVERCOME

By turning to the practice approach for revising the unit of analysis, we aim to dissolve two persistent dichotomies in the social sciences related to the formation of human conduct: the division between the individual and the societal and that between the organism and environmental determination of conduct.

The Division between Individual and Society

We want to tear down the boundary conceived of in the idea of determination of human conduct either by societal and organizational structures or by individuals' intentions (see Figure 2.1). This society/individual dualism is reflected in the name often given to the discipline: human and organizational factors. The human-factors discipline may acknowledge the need to tackle both aspects, but, in fact, it typically focuses on only one or the other. For example, Kenneth Pettersen et al. (2010, p. 185) claimed that the cognitive and social cognitive approaches that are dominant in work on human factors in socio-technical systems focus on the intentional element but rarely address the structural properties of the system. The latter are the explicit concern of the organizational design and management (ODAM) movement (Wilson, 2014; Zink, 2014) and macroergonomics (Carayon et al., 2014; Kleiner, 2006).

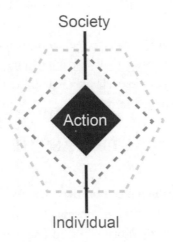

Figure 2.1: It is proposed that the dichotomy between individual-level and societal (structural) determination of activity as viewed by human-factors research be dissolved via redefinition of the unit of analysis, moving it from action to practice. The dashed lines portray the anticipated expansion of the unit of analysis.

The ODAM and macroergonomic approaches are grounded in socio-technical systems theory, which clearly offers prospects for viewing the design of complex work systems with a lens focused on production, well-being, and sustainability. Socio-technical systems theory is known for its pioneering shift of emphasis to the group as the primary unit of analysis (Walker et al., 2007). This proposed redefinition of the unit of analysis is well motivated when one considers the systemic nature of the problems to be overcome in modern work. The proposed shift is from one level of a system (i.e., the individual) to other levels (i.e., those of the group and organization). The authors cited explain, further, that the socio-technical systems approach takes the concepts and metaphors of general systems theory, especially the notion of "open system," as a way of describing, analyzing, and designing systems with joint optimization of their performance in mind. For us, the socio-technical design approaches are clearly focused on organizations within which the various elements and their interactions are treated from a structural point of view. The intentions of individuals that are manifested in the ways people act in their daily work are not given the focus; it is placed instead on the effect actions have for the optimal behavior of the system. On account of these features, we consider this theoretical approach to represent the idea of structural determination of human conduct.

Our proposal to adopt practice as the new unit of analysis is the means of bridging the gap between organizational and intentional determination, an aim shared by many practice theorists (Nicolini, 2013, pp. 44-76). This proposal is supported by the ideas of Yolande Pierce and colleagues, who work within the HCI community. They note that, because of the systemic nature of the current problems of work and everyday life, such as those connected to sustainability, and the limits to the capacity of individuals' action to solve them, there is a need to intervene at multiple scales. The authors state that the prospects for intervening at other levels than the individual's are, however, unclear, at least given current HCI methodology. Instead, Pierce et al. suggested shifting the main unit of analysis from individuals' action to everyday practice (Pierce et al., 2013, pp. 1-2).

In the cultural-historical theory of activity, the interplay between individual-level and societal-level determination of activity is addressed by the concept of activity system proposed by Engeström (1987). This concept was developed on the basis of the activity concept of Lev Vygotsky (1978) and Alexei Leont'ev (1978). The original concept was tuned to individuals' activity even though Leont'ev in particular emphasized that individual-level activity assumes considering said activity's collective nature arising from the historical process of division of labor. Engeström's contribution was to make the social nature of human activity even more explicit and to expound on the material and symbolic mediations that give activity a networked-system-like structure. Engeström's activity-system concept has been applied widely as the key concept of the developmental work research school (Sannino et al., 2009).

The Division between Organism and Environment

The second dichotomy to be alleviated is the one between organism and environment (see Figure 2.2). The two are currently considered to be separate elements. Their interaction is dealt with as information flow between two elements, with processing of information on the environment in the human brain being one possible perspective. This is a feasible concept for application, but it tends to draw attention to the internal structure of the two "elements" and cannot explain the content of the relationship between these elements and its meaning. How, then, could we tackle the "teamwork" between the human and the technical plus environmental elements in a manner that yields better understanding of the meaning of such processing?

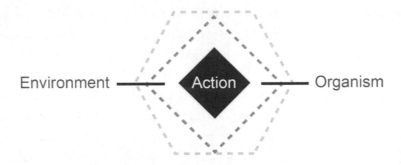

Figure 2.2: It is proposed that the dichotomy between the organism and the environment in the determination of activity as viewed by human-factors research be dissolved via redefinition of the unit of analysis, moving it from action to practice. The dashed lines portray the anticipated expansion of the unit of analysis.

A monistic approach has been proposed that focuses on the functions that certain parts of the human organism and the environment accomplish together for reaching of goals that are beneficial for the viability of the organism–environment system in certain circumstances (Ingold, 2000, pp. 18-19; Järvilehto, 1998). The organism–environment joint-system approach that adherents to this school of thought represent draws on the idea of functional units of the organism and environment. Herein, tools are considered to be elements in the environment that serve certain functions: "Perceiving is activity in which the organism fastens to parts of the environment and, thus, divides it into objects and tools that are appropriate for his purposes" (Järvilehto, 1994, p. 139).

Of the practice-theory approaches, those focusing on the embodiment of practices in the body and material things would support a monist notion of the organism–environment relationship. For example, it is clearly identifiable in the thoughts of Bourdieu, who with the notion of *habitus* highlights a set of mental dispositions, bodily schemata, and skills operating at a preconscious level. The schemata are seen as activated by events in the fields of practices (Bourdieu, 1990, p. 73). Here, Bourdieu's connections to Merleau-Ponty and Michael Polanyi become visible. The corporeal schemata (i.e., habits) allow the sedimentation of past activity so enable new ways of understanding and acting (Merleau-Ponty, 1986, pp.164-166). A range of capabilities for action becomes realized only within the action that it makes possible.

The idea of the functional unity of the human organism and the environment is central also to the thinking of Dewey (2002) and Peirce (1958).[3] In the recent history of psychology, it is

---

[3]   Much earlier philosophical background for this idea is provided by the philosopher Baruch Spinoza, who, in opposition to René Descartes, strongly argued for a unity of the soul and body, and of the human and environment, and emphasized the capability for activity as a central characteristic of nature. Also, in the philosophy of Karl Marx, practice is a central category expressing the relationship between human and environment and explaining the transformative and epistemic power of humans.

James Gibson's (1979) ideas of perception in his ecological psychology and Ulrich Neisser's (1976) ecological approach to cognitive processes as a continuous cycle between the human and the environment that support a monistic approach. In recent human-factors discussion, Kevin Bennett and John Flach (2011) have strongly advocated taking such an ecological notion as the basis of human factors in interface design. Among other current authors, Erik Hollnagel and David Woods, two well-known experts in cognitive engineering, support a monistic approach through their concept of the joint cognitive system (Hollnagel and Woods, 2005; Woods and Hollnagel, 2006).

How to Overcome the Unnecessary Distinctions

The two dichotomies with regard to which we redefine the unit of analysis are made explicit in Figures 2.1 and 2.2. Further, Figure 2.3 illustrates how the unit of analysis can be cross-illuminated via consideration of both the individual-level (intentional)—societal (structural) dimension and the organism–environment dichotomy in the analysis of practice.

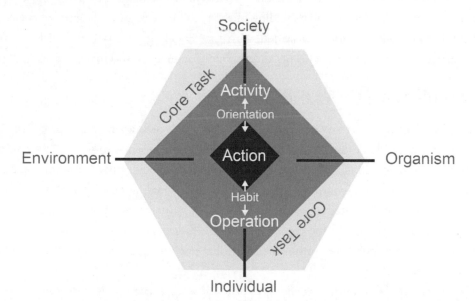

Figure 2.3: Practice as the unit of analysis in the Core-Task Design approach. The traditional unit of analysis in human factors research (i.e., individual action) is depicted in the middle. The redefinition takes place with regard to the individual–society dichotomy and the organism–environment dichotomy. Practice is operationalized through several concepts: the core task indicated by the light grey hexagon is modeled with regard to both dichotomies (see Section 2.2.2); the larger diamond around "Action" refers to real-world actual activity that is conceptualized in terms of the hierarchical notion of activity (see Section 2.2.3).

The intended change in the unit of analysis may also be interpreted in such a manner that the individual action as the traditional unit of analysis is contextualized with regard to both the society and the environment. We consider any situation to present possibilities and constraints that the actors are inclined or willing to actualize or take into account, respectively. The contextualization is achieved by defining the core task of the activity. The core task portrays acting from a generic and possible, not specific and actual point of view. Those following the CTD approach are interested in ascertaining the principles and dynamics according to which the realization of the possibilities takes place. For comprehension of the core task, two distinct types of models are used: the **activity-system model** and the **core-task functions model** (see Section 2.2.2).

Real-world **actual activity** is considered as a hierarchical entity with the levels of **activity**, **action**, and **operation**. The **orientation** mechanisms (orientation and habit) describe the connections between the levels. The concepts used in analysis of activity are depicted by the diamonds in the middle of Figure 2.3. In analysis of the real-world activity, we discover how the contextual possibilities and constraints are taken into account by the actors. Via analysis of the actual activity, it is possible to elaborate further the understanding of the possibilities and constraints of the core task.

Next, CTD methodology is presented, with the modeling approaches used to capture the core task described first. Then, the concepts and methods for analysis of actual activity are explicated.

2.2.2 CORE-TASK MODELING

The possibilities for activity emerge in the context in which acting takes place. The context is defined relative to the individual–society and the organism–environment dichotomies. This whole determines the core task. Modeling methods designed specifically to conceptualize the core task cover the light grey hexagon in Figure 2.3. Core-task modeling enables analysis of the actual activity, but, as already indicated, the actual activity always increases knowledge of the core task and may also produce change in the core task. The core-task perspective on activity is adopted for understanding of the possibilities within the individual–society perspective and the organism–environment perspective.

The core task is the generic developing of content of the work and expresses itself as joint functions emerging from the meeting of the human organism's resources with the possibilities and constraints of the environment for reaching certain global objectives of work activity.

The concept of the core task forces specification of the object of activity through consideration of the functions that the human–environment system needs to fulfill for tackling the object of activity in an appropriate way. The core task determines how the human and the environment can become organized so as to work together in a certain context or work domain. The core task is identified in a functional description of the task; i.e., the environmental and social features are defined from the perspective of what use they could offer for the human, and the human capabilities are defined from the perspective of what is required to make the environment useful and meaningful.

The core task is not always clear to the actors, with one reason being that the generic content of the work is manifested in various forms in the concrete daily work. Another reason for insufficient comprehension of the core task is that when changes occur in the work, the content of the core task too may change. Therefore, comprehending the core task may necessitate analysis and recurrent reflection. By making the core task explicit, one makes evident what is the object and meaningful core of the work, on which to focus (Norros, 2004, pp.17-18; Norros and Nuutinen, 2002). In the following. three modeling methods for defining the core task will be introduced.

The Activity-System Model

The activity-system concept of CHAT is the most appropriate framework we have encountered for conceptualization of work from the structural and at the same time the intentional perspective. It enables comprehending the activity of an organization and of people in that organization at the same time. The activity system approach is a holistic system-oriented approach.

The activity system concept has been represented as a triangle; see Figure 2.4 below. According to the model, three basic elements can be identified first: the actor, community, and object of activity (Engeström, 1987). The fundamental principle that provides a structure for the activity system is that the relationships among the first three elements are mediated by three further elements, shown in Figure 2.4: tools and concepts are needed to maintain relationships between the actor and the object of activity. Rules and norms enable individual actors to interact with the community of which they are a part. Division of labor takes the role of organizing the community to act upon the object of work. It is precisely these mediating elements that make the activity social.

The elements of the activity are integrated into a whole by the **object of activity**. The object has the primary role in shaping the characteristics of the relationships within the entire activity system. This is due to the potential of an object to motivate activity and to suggest purposes for acting. Furthermore, the object of activity is always bundled with particular constraints that need to be taken into account in the actual process via which the object is transformed into the outcomes of activity (Leont'ev, 1978); this transformation process is represented in the model by the horizontal arrow from the object to the outcome. At the same time, demands as to the quality of the outcome put pressure on the activity system, hence the horizontal arrow from outcome to object. An important idea under the activity-system concept is that there are contradictions within and between elements of the system, and there is resistance to change. Finally, a particular activity system may also exhibit disconnects with other activity systems in a network of systems. Together, the contradictions and resistance are considered the source of change in the system.

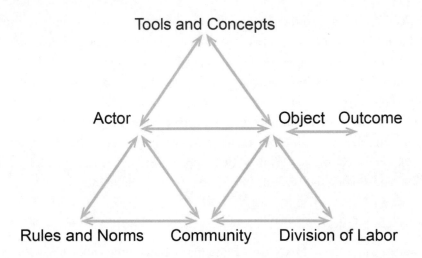

Figure 2.4: Activity as a system of interacting elements. The elements of the system are integrated by the object of activity and the aimed outcome (Engeström, 1987).

Via the activity-system concept, it is possible to analyze the role of technology in the behavior of individuals (and teams) in connection with the social structures that an organization or a system of organizations provides. The structure constrains the activity in question, but it is also reproduced by that activity. The activity-system approach and its benefits for human–computer interaction research have been discussed extensively by Victor Kaptelinin and Bonnie Nardi (2012; 2006).

The activity-system perspective is unique among system-oriented approaches in its exploitation of the concept of activity. As is indicated above, this concept explains the meaning of activity as emerging from the concrete content of the object of activity, and the relationships between the various elements are elaborated upon under this concept via the notion of mediation. Adoption of the concept of activity (or practice) constitutes the fundamental difference between Core-Task Design and those human-factors approaches that draw directly from systems theory. The latter also go beyond the individual-action perspective and include organizational, technological, and individual-task elements in the analysis, but do not exploit the concept of activity to conceptualize the connections between the elements. Examples of the systems-theory-oriented approaches include the systems engineering initiative for patient safety model (SEIPS), described by P. Carayon (2006), Carayon et al. (2014), and Brian M. Kleiner (2006), and the systemic human-factors analysis of John Wilson (2014). When drawing on systems theory, adherents to these approaches explain the organization of systems and the connections between the elements of them via abstract concepts from systems theory. The challenge of system-theory-oriented human-factors analysis, as Wilson noted, is that one deals with the constituent parts rather than being holistic (2014, p. 12).

Its utility notwithstanding, the activity-system approach might also place too much emphasis on the structural determination of human conduct in its leaning toward systems theory and, it has been pointed out, may thereby neglect the process perspective and the intentions of individuals. Another critical point that could be raised is that this approach strongly emphasizes goal-oriented rational aspects of human conduct (Nicolini, 2013, pp. 119-120). In recognition of these concerns, we redefine the unit of analysis via the organism–environment perspective and give more focus to the analysis of real-world activity in real-world situations, as will become evident in the next sections.

The Core-Task Functions Model

For balance to the potentially excessive emphasis on structural determination brought in by application of the activity-system model, we draw on practice-theory approaches highlighting the embodied aspects of the human conduct. This perspective assumes conceiving of activity from the organism–environment perspective (the horizontal dichotomy depicted in Figure 2.2). The idea here is to create bridges that break down dualism, in this case between the organism and the environment, which is possible through adoption of a monist organism–environment system point of view.

From the organism–environment perspective, we consider practice to be a joint function composed of parts of the environment and parts of the human. We have concretized the idea of a joint system by describing each element from the perspective of the other. Hence, we describe the environment from the point of view of the human organism, i.e., we clarify what possibilities for action the environment enables with respect to what he or she is aiming to do and we ascertain what constraints it imposes on action. There must exist complementary human sensitivity and capability to tune to and grasp the environment's possibilities and to take into account the constraints. Capabilities of becoming part of the environment are art-specific and culturally produced. We understand, in line with Tim Ingold's thinking, that both the features of the environment as possibilities and constraints and features of the human organism's resources for acting emerge in the life process itself (Ingold, 2000, p. 19). They do not exist as independent "givens." We also remember that they are continuously shaped, especially by developing technology.

Practical means are needed for clarifying the mutual interaction of the organism and the environment. For this purpose, we created an illustrative but also conceptually coherent framework. The model defines the interaction by bringing together the conceptualization of the environmental possibilities and constraints and the human resources, to enable harnessing the possibilities and rendering the environment a meaningful object. Drawing on the literature regarding the inherent characteristics of various work domains, we analyze the possibilities and constraints with the aid of three generic system features: **dynamism, complexity**, and **uncertainty** (Norros, 2004; Vicente, 1999; Woods, 1988). People working in the domain define these features for themselves when they grasp them, equipped as they are with certain resources for action. We group the resources for acting into three classes: pragmatic resources, i.e., skills; epistemic resources, i.e., knowledge; and heuristic resources, i.e., collaboration that includes self-reflection. Arguments for use of these three categories may be found in, for example, the work of Pierre Rabardel, a knowledgeable advocate of activity theory (Norros, 2004; Rabardel and Duvenci-Langa, 2002).

When the possibilities and constraints of the domain and the human resources meet, nine types of joint functions between human and environment emerge. We call these *core-task functions* and consider them to represent the central content or demands of the work and, thereby, to define the core task. These functions need to be maintained in all situations if high quality of work is to be produced. High work quality means not only the external targets for the work being reached well but also achieving the internal good of the profession. It is clear that in complex work including uncertainties, high-quality external output is not a sufficiently sensitive indication of mastery of the work. Here we draw on Alasdair MacIntyre's notion of the good of the practice (MacIntyre, 1984), which denotes the practitioner community's own understanding of what characterizes good work and the professional ethos (Norros, 2004; 2014, p. 202).

The modeling method is depicted in Figure 2.5. The model consists of two intersecting triangles, one symbolizing the environment and the other the human organism. The model highlights "hot spots" where each of the three environmental or human elements comes together with the other triangle. These are the core-task functions, composed of environmental and human elements working together. The functions are viewed from the perspective of each human resource for acting. For example, skills enable coping with dynamism, with resultant readiness to act; skills also enable coping with uncertainty, thereby fulfilling the functions of narrowing of options and testing; and, finally, skills enable coping with complexity and thereby lead to the function of focusing on what is critical. Corresponding reasoning with regard to the resources of knowledge results in the functions of perceiving of weak signals and anticipating, interpreting and reorienting, and mastery of concepts and comprehension of wholes. When one sets the resources of collaboration and reflection in relation to the three classes of possibilities and constraints, the functions of optimal sharing of efforts, dialog for creation of knowledge, and creation of shared awareness emerge (as shown in Figure 2.5). Once the skill-, knowing-, and collaboration- and reflection-related core-task functions of a particular activity have been identified, it is possible to infer what specific resources for acting should be developed for the work through various educational, selection, or design measures so that these core-task functions (or demands) may be realized by the personnel.

The model in Figure 2.5 is a generic core-task function model for process-control-type work, which has traditionally been characterized in human-factors research on the basis of generic categories summarized here as dynamism, complexity, and uncertainty (see for example, Vicente, 1999, pp. 14-17). We consider, however, that these generic features may be relevant in characterisation of many other work activities in the modern world. A recent example of the use of core-task function modeling comes from the maritime domain. In this example, the authors developed concrete descriptions for the nine core-task functions and used them as the design goals in creation of a new ship-bridge concept (Wahlström et al., accepted for publication).

In empirical analysis of any particular work with the aid of the core-task function model, various kinds of empirical data are used and concretization of the abstract model in Figure 2.5 is achieved. This concretization proceeds from describing what kinds of temporal features of dynamism, which elements bringing uncertainty, or the number and type of connections creating complexity the work may entail. The core-task functions, concretized with regard to the specific features of each domain, are later used as a contextual reference in the empirical analysis and evaluation of real activity.

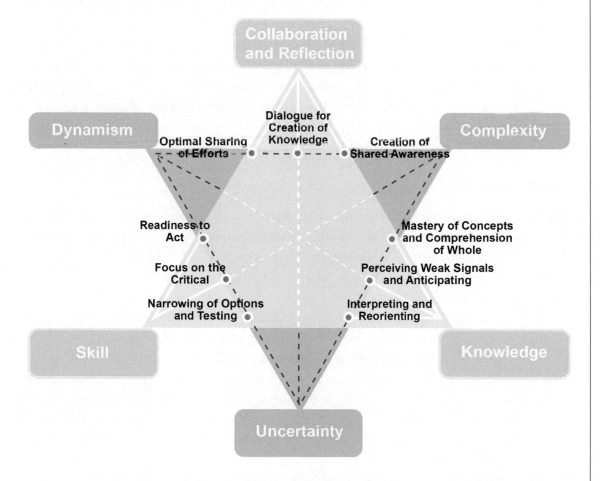

Figure 2.5: Core-task functions of process-control-type work in complex, dynamic, and uncertain environments. The core-task functions (marked with dots) emerge when human resources of skills, knowledge, and collaboration and reflection are mobilized for purposes of grasping dynamism, uncertainty, or complexity features of the domain.

The core-task function modeling employed has connections to the abstraction hierarchy modeling approach proposed by Jens Rasmussen for functional modeling of the control demands of industrial processes from a means–end-based perspective (Rasmussen, 1986). Hence, the domain features that we describe under the headings of dynamism, complexity, and uncertainty could—in the abstraction hierarchy frame—be interpreted as "abstract functions," means to maintain the "functional meaning" of the domain (e.g., safety), and they can be broken down into "generic functions" that realize them (i.e., the core-task functions). The core-task functions are populated by data from each domain studied, which descriptions represent the lower levels of Rasmussen's abstraction hierarchy.

Clearly, in contrast to the Rasmussen modeling approach, our functional modeling deals with a joint human–environment system and considers the means–ends functions composed of both human and domain elements. In the original writings of Rasmussen, this interpretation was not excluded. In later refinement of the Rasmussen model, a strong opinion is expressed that the modeling focuses on the domain (Naikar, 2013, pp. 139-149; Vicente, 1999, Chapter 7). The analysis of human activity is, accordingly, left to later phases of Cognitive Work Analysis. Because cognitively oriented concepts are exploited there, the connection to the context analyzed well by means of domain modeling is loosened in explaining human operator behavior.

Functional Situation Modeling

With the CTD approach, we are interested in the details of how the joint organism–environment system functions in specific situations, and we consider situations to be instances of the core-task functions. The situations are temporal and spatial phenomena in which the joint system is actualized. Indeed, the concept of situation can be interpreted to correspond to the notion of human–environment system (Järvilehto, 1994, p. 50).

Although situations are real in their own right, it is necessary to have a method to describe them from the perspective of the possibilities and constraints they provide with respect to action. Situational models have been developed by theorists such as Flach et al. (2004), who offer a theory-based depiction of how Rasmussen's levels of abstraction could be used to describe resources within situations. Johannes Petersen (2004) also developed modeling in order to understand control situations for the purpose of design of human–machine systems. More recently, Cato Alexander Bjørkli et al. (2007) added the level of strategy to Petersen's model on the basis of empirical work in a maritime environment.

Our modeling of situations too has a basis in Rasmussen's ideas. An earlier version of the modeling method (Norros, 2004, pp. 114-120) laid the foundations for the present one, labeled functional situation modeling, or FSM (Savioja, 2014; Savioja et al., 2012a). The models require a great deal of understanding of the context and are always developed in collaboration with domain experts. These models represent both a task- and a function-oriented view of the relevant situation and represent a potential instance of the joint functioning of the human actors and the domain.

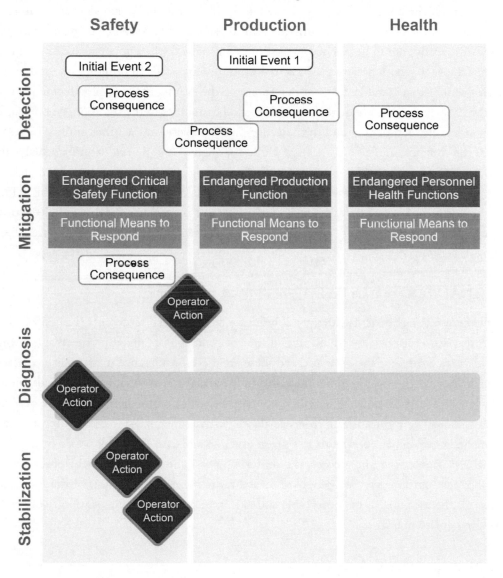

Figure 2.6: The basic structure of a functional situation model. The model represents a particular instance of the joint organism–environment system and is constructed to serve as a reference for understanding the meaning of concrete actions in real-world situations. The model combines a task-oriented view (vertical) with a function-based view (horizontal) of an activity in a situation, and makes explicit how certain initial events threaten the functions and what means and operator actions can recover the lost functions or maintain threatened ones.

The generic template for creation of the model is depicted in Figure 2.6 (Savioja et al., 2012a). The task view includes the main phases of an activity in a particular control task (along the vertical axis in the figure). The horizontal axis in Figure 2.6 represents the functional view and features the main objectives of the activity. We identify the critical functions that need to be maintained if the objectives of the work are to be reached in the situation studied, wherein particular process events have been actualized. The functions are broken down into technical and other means, and in terms of operator actions that could be relevant as response to the events. The modeling technique makes evident the connection from the actual constraints and possibilities in the situation, on one hand, to the upper-level control functions and the objectives of the activity, on the other. It must be remembered that the situation models are means to aid in the analysis and do not describe actual activity.

We have completed many simulator studies, in a range of domains. Situation models have been used in the preparation of the runs and in the analysis of action. In studies in the wild, situations are not predefined as they are in simulation-based studies, but models can be constructed after the events with the aim of identifying the possibilities for action that were available for exercising in action.

2.2.3   ANALYSIS OF ACTUAL ACTIVITY

While the core task circumscribes the possibilities for action, it also represents the context for action with regard to the society–individual and the environment–organism perspective (see Figure 2.3). Models are created of the core task, and these are used for reference in analysis of the **actual activity**. The two perspectives become integrated in the actual activity that is the focus of our analysis. Our analysis of the actual activity is not, however, restricted to the immediately observable individual actions; we want, instead, to reveal the underlying mechanisms of activity that explain the nature and development of actions in a given situation and over time. This we do by asking and observing *how* people take into account the contextual possibilities, not merely by observing *what* they do. For that purpose, we have proposed several further concepts. Analysis of the *how* mechanisms reveals the meaning of the observable and aids in understanding the continuity of action in the changing environment.

Activity, Action, and Operation

In our attempts to understand the actual activity, we exploit the activity concept of Leont'ev (Leont'ev, 1978, pp. 62-74). Through comprehensive historical analysis of the development of human conduct, he demonstrated that activity has a hierarchical structure (Leontjew, 1973). The structure comprises three main levels: *activity*, *action*, and *operation*.

The basic unit that expresses the subject's relationship to the environment is the object of activity. It is that part of the environment that offers possibilities and becomes meaningful for the subject forming the motive for the activity. In the course of history, as the activities of human actors grew more complex and division of labor emerged, the object motivating activity and the object toward which an actor oriented the self in specific situations in a series of **actions** began to diverge. As a result, actions are oriented toward a goal and only indirectly toward the motive. Actions, for their part, also become divided into smaller units, called **operations**, that in a routine-like way provide orientation to the conditions the environment imposes for realization of actions. We assume that the operations too must maintain a connection to the motive if they are to be meaningful. Furthermore, we interpret Leont'ev's concept of orientation from a pragmatist perspective and see orientation as building of beliefs of the world that appear both as mental and bodily practices.

In the analysis of activity, we start by identifying actions as sequences of observable behaviors and events. Our empirical data collection exploits standard ethnographic methods of observation, self-reporting, or interviews for compiling data on actors' behavior and accounts of their actions. Said data are used to analyze movements, operations, performance, efforts to provide the performance, and explanations for actions. Representational tools of various sorts are used in the analysis and for summarizing the results.

Orientation and Habit

As we have noted, we are also interested in what generic, more stable mechanisms lie behind the actions, the "how" mechanisms. We are especially interested in the processes of orientation in situations. According to the theory of Leont'ev, orientations are behavior-directing mechanisms that establish connections between the goal-directed tasks and the motive, and between the condition-driven operations and the goal along with the underlying motive (see Figure 2.3). Orientation describes the personal sense of acting in an activity system.

In situational acting, the motive for the activity and the core task are only indirectly present, on account of division of labor and also the spatial and temporal structuring of the activity. We term the orientation mechanism that mediates between the goal and motive simply *(work) orientation* (again, see Figure 2.3). This orientation mechanism is defined as *personal definition of the goal of action expressing the stance with relation to the object of activity and its societal meaning, manifested in the core task* (slightly adapted from Norros, 2004, p. 13). We consider actors able to make their work orientation explicit, and we have developed interviews for enquiring into this. In connection with the practice-theory approach, this mechanism appears resonant with the assumption that practices are accountable and serve sense-making, and that they are open to mediation by natural language. Accordingly, we try to discover how strongly the actor maintains the general motive of the activity while acting in specific situations, what the actor's stance is to the object of work, and how the motive and the core task support sense-making in actual situations. We may also discover that the contents of the motive and core task may become redefined by the actors on the basis of experience of real-world situations.

The second orientation mechanism becomes evident in bodily practices and is the routine-like orienting to the conditions of the environment. It is the mechanism that mediates between goals and the conditions. We interpreted Leont'ev such that the orienting toward the conditions must be connected to the motive, although in an indirect way. The tacit or embodied nature of routine orientation impedes identification of the relationship to the motive. We consider this orienting mechanism to be *habit* (see Figure 2.3). In empirical analysis, we identify habits in the form of *habits of action*, *habits of knowing*, and *habits of collaboration*, corresponding to the human organism's resources and the core-task functions connected to them. In general descriptions, we may employ the idea of *way of acting* when not distinguishing among the types of habit. Habits, as work orientation does, express the personal sense of acting in the situation. We may note that this embodied orientation mechanism corresponds with one of the basic assumptions of ethnomethodology—i.e., indexicality, under which meaning is embedded in practical action. It goes further in stating that the stability of sense, relevance, and meaning arises not from the form of propositions but from the circumstances of their use.

The idea of an embodied routine-like orienting mechanism is particularly typical of American pragmatist thinking. The concept of habit that we exploit is borrowed from this tradition: *habit is generic readiness or potential to grasp the possibilities of the environment and to act successfully in a certain environment* (Dewey, 2002; Peirce, 1998b). According to Peirce, habit is a mechanism with which a human actor can anticipate the results of his or her actions in a given environment. This mechanism assumes certain associations, whose focus is not merely on perceptions of the environment. Instead, associations cover also series of actions as mechanism that control actions such that they correspond adequately to the perceived environ-mental constraints. Via this mechanism, the features of the environment become meaningful for the human, and continuity between the human and his or her environment is established (Määttänen, 2009, pp. 88-98).

In our manner of exploiting the concept of habit, we draw on the triadic semiotic model of habit proposed by Peirce (1958). This model is depicted in Figure 2.7.

The model proposes a mechanism by which the human in his or her action makes sense of the environment. The *object* in the model refers to a material or ideal target in the environment. The *sign* is a cue that refers to this object of acting. The *interpretant* represents operations that realize action (physical or in thought or emotion), and it demonstrates that a connection exists between the sign and the object. In its logic, making sense of the environment follows a reasoning process that is termed *abductive* reasoning, characteristic of which is that, while one acts on the environment and observes signs, guesses and assumptions surrounding the object emerge ("could it be that …?"). These insights are tested in practical action in a continuous process. Consequently, beliefs about the environment emerge. These are habits (Norros, 2004, pp. 70-83; Peirce, 1998c, pp. 226-241).

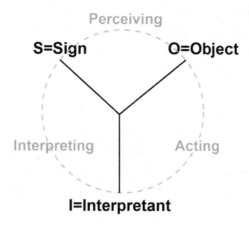

Figure 2.7: The triadic semiotic model of habit presented by Peirce. A continuous perception—interpreting—acting cycle can be seen to take place within the semiotic structure and to produce habit (as illustrated by Määttänen, 2009). This cycle is indicated in the background of the figure.

As fruit of the functioning of this mechanism, habits emerge that represent a form of generalization and are a source of generic knowledge of the environment. They are stable and repetitive in their capability to support anticipation of results of one's action in an uncertain world, and in the meaning they convey. Also taken into consideration is that, when the object (i.e., the environment) shows resistance—that is, when the environment does not mesh with the expectations built in the habit—the habit must be tuned or changed. This creates the possibility of "reflective habituality" (Joas, 1996), which also forms the core for creation of knowledge.

A Semiotic Model of Habit as a Tool of Empirical Analysis

In the analysis of concrete action, we identify critical courses of action (i.e., episodes), from which we analyze how actors make sense of the situation. This is done by looking into the three elements of habit in greater depth. We then discover that actors respond differently to the environment and build different beliefs about the situation in their action, knowing, or collaboration. The next step in the analysis is to characterize the differences (an example is discussed in Chapter 3).

To comprehend the various responses that emerge from the empirical material, we exploit the Peircean theory of abduction and consider the responses to express more or less strong *inter*pretation—i.e., creation of knowledge and generalization—of the situation. The grading draws on the Peircean idea of several epistemic relationships a human being may have to the reality: There is, first, a perceptual response, which is positive but reactive; it remains restricted to itself. The second relationship, which we have termed a confirmative relationship, is one in which the perception of an event has a connection to a necessary counterpart but, in the absence of reference to something further, nothing more. The third relationship is interpretative. This refers to connecting the perception of an event, with the necessary response, to something further, a third element—i.e., an object that gives the meaning for both and whereby also the adequacy of the connection between the two may be tested. A developed habit has this triadic nature (Peirce, 1998d, pp. 268-288), and the more sensitive the habit is to variance in the object and to the possible resistance of an object, the stronger the interpretation- and knowledge-creating power of the habit (reflective habituality).

We illustrate the three distinct relationships described above with Figure 2.8. In the figure, the reactive relationship is expressed by the sign alone, indicating that it already includes the operational response. The confirmative relationship has two elements, expressing an unambiguous connection of the signal and an operation. The interpretative relationship is a triadic one, with the sign and the operation via which it is connected to a third element, in the environment. Because of the connection to the environment, there is a possibility of continuous testing of the operation such that it can become more and more appropriate relative to the environment.

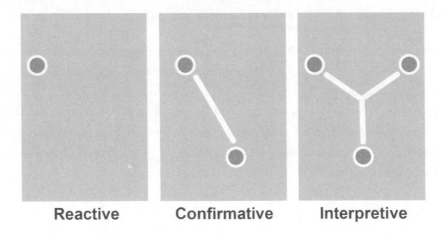

Figure 2.8: An illustration of the three basic epistemic attitudes to the environment: in the reactive relationship, the sign encompasses the reaction, the confirmative relationship is characterized by an unambiguous connection between sign and reaction, and in the triadic, i.e., interpretative, relationship the sign is connected to an object in the environment via an interpretative reaction.

Even though use of the concept of habit is not very frequent in current human-factors research, there are other important examples of its successful use.[4] Recent interest in the schema

---

4   The triadic model of sign (or habit) is used by Bennett and Flach (2011) in their approach to interface design. Addressing the human factors of safety-critical domains, Pettersen (2013) draws on the Peircean idea of abductive thinking in theorizing about how to conceptualize the role of procedures in action. Also, in their analysis of high reliability organisations, Weick and Sutcliffe (2007) display a connection to the habit conception in their description of the process of sense-making.

theories can also be observed as a sign of the need for macro-cognitive concepts through the lens of which to analyze human conduct (Plant and Stanton, 2013). Our semiotic analysis of habit as the unit of sense-making in natural situations is clearly one example of pursuing this aim.

Functions of a Tool in Activity

In organism–environment system thinking, it is assumed that in activity the environment is structured into objects of activity and tools that become parts of the system. Since we are interested in the design of tools and try to support the design such that the tools would be as appropriate as possible for the activity, we need a way to determine what is required of a good tool. Our idea is that the definition of "good" should be based on the generic role that a tool plays in human activity. In examining this issue, we exploit one of the main principles of activity theory, that of mediation. We turn to Vygotsky (1978), who explained the basic role of a tool or sign in activity. Accordingly, we identify three functions of a tool: the **instrumental**, **psychological**, and **communicative** functions (Savioja and Norros, 2008, 2012).

Via its instrumental function, technology is rendered capable of influencing the environment in line with the actors' intentions. For example, one of the most widely used tools today, the mobile phone, in combination with the wireless networks that provide infrastructure for this tool, serves in an instrumental function as it enables mobile connectedness among people.

The psychological function of a tool refers to the possibility of external control and development of behavior that tools, including concepts, enable. Vygotsky notes that "tying a knot as a reminder is one example of a pervasive regulatory principle of human behavior, i.e., *signification*, wherein people create temporary links and give significance to previously neutral stimuli in the context of their problem-solving efforts. We regard our method as important because it helps to *objectify* inner psychological processes" (Vygotsky, 1978, p. 74). Through creation of such external links, or auxiliary stimuli, in the learning environment, it is possible to improve learning greatly and to involve learners in development of the activity (Engeström, 2011). Working from the idea of the psychological function of a tool, Pierre Rabardel and Pascal Béguin (2005) developed their theory of instrument genesis. They point out that without development of the links described between the user, the tool, and the environment, the ostensible tool is not actually a tool at all. In CTD, we draw extensively from the idea of the psychological function of a tool when arguing that there is necessity of understanding the developing of competencies and skills of the end users as an integral part of the design of the technology to be implemented.

In moving beyond the instrumental and psychological functions of a tool to consider the third function mentioned above, we look to the proposed connections between CHAT and media theories (Rückriem, 2009). With the communicative function, the role of the tool as a medium, or a vehicle of development of collaborative social activity and shared meaning, is highlighted.

The mobile phone functions as a communication tool because many people have appropriated its use, and they know who uses it, what to expect when using it, and the "correct" etiquette of use. Specific to a medium is that it is not defined by serving a preordained purpose. Rather, a medium, such as photography or augmented reality (AR), is a generic mode of influencing people and involving people in action. A medium is effective through being coupled with the human senses, and it extends the power of the natural senses. In this way, the medium is directly incorporated into sense-making. The dominant message of a medium is how it affects the human actors' acting, not the content that it typically carries. For example, AR is a medium for the new dimension of perception it enables, which gradually will be expected of the environment and only secondarily via the content that it provides—for instance, projecting assembly instructions directly onto an object undergoing maintenance.

Definition of what constitutes a good tool starts with the claim that a good tool needs to fulfill the functions described above for a tool. The more comprehensively the tool supports these functions, the better it is as a tool. But how should we identify the actual goodness of the tool? Evidently, this can be done through observation of activity of using the tool and considering how the tool supports mastery of the object of activity and the core task. Hence, one may observe first how well the **actions are performed**, with the reference being various kinds of outcome criteria, such as the time taken, error count, and the smoothness of operations. Indeed, this seems to be the reference that usability evaluations typically exploit. As the core-task approach also identifies the **way of acting**—i.e., the underlying relatively stable way of acting that expresses the meaning of actions with regard to fulfilling the core-task functions that the tool should support—we may legitimately refer to this perspective. Finally, the tool has a capability to facilitate possibilities for activity in the environment and to make sense of it. From the pragmatist view, the experience of the tool emerges from connecting it to the activity and identifying the possibilities that it may provide to reach intended outcomes. Hence, the associated perspective, that of **user experience**, can be included (Wright and McCarthy, 2010, have extensively elaborated on this possibility). We exploit as a reference for good experience an idea of Vygotsky, that positive emotions emerge when new mediation in activity is created that promises development of the activity (Koski-Jännes, 1999).

When the principles of activity being mediated and object-oriented are taken into account, through combination of the three functions of a tool and the three perspectives on activity, a new way to express what constitutes an appropriate tool emerges. The attribute of being a good tool has been labeled *systems usability* (Savioja and Norros, 2012). One could state that *systems usability denotes the capability of the technology to fulfill the instrumental, psychological, and communicative functions of a tool in the activity and to support fulfillment of the core-task functions in the work. Systems usability is evidenced in technology's usage by an appropriate performance outcome, way of acting, and user experience* (adapted from Savioja, 2014, p.87).

The two dimensions, tools' functions and the perspectives on activity, enable constructing a conceptual grid with nine cells, each expressing a specific characteristic of systems usability that emerges from the combination of the tool function and the perspective on activity. Each cell is an indicator with a descriptive name that characterizes the principal content of the cell. Figure 2.9 depicts this systems-usability grid and the emerging general indicators of systems usability, modified slightly from earlier work (Savioja and Norros, 2012). Under each general indicator, examples of concrete indicators and measures for systems usability may be developed (see Chapter 4).

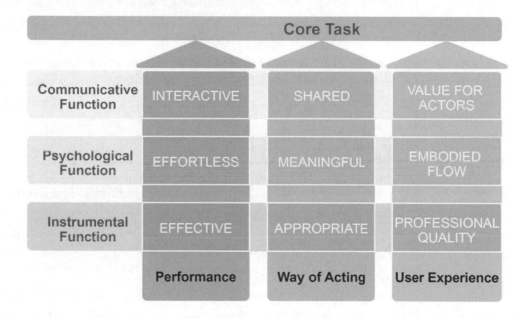

Figure 2.9: The nine general indicators of systems usability. These emerge when the three tool functions are connected to the three perspectives on activity.

We are currently developing procedures for exploiting the SU concept as a tool in design. It appears that the concept could be helpful in the various phases of design, from concept design through to evaluation of the tool for acceptance into regular use. Through the aid of the SU concept, it could be possible to steer the design and confirm that the end product fulfills the generic criteria for SU. With this in mind, we came to the idea of exploiting the case-based reasoning that is currently used in arguing for or against the safety of various complex systems (Bishop and Bloomfield, 1998). A so-called safety case is required by many safety standards (ONR, 2014). Establishment of a safety case is aimed at making explicit the evidence pertaining to the technology or organization that can be argued to endanger or support safety. In a safety case, the safety consequences of design decisions about the technology can be made traceable over the life cycle of a plant. Since this aim is relevant also with respect to human-factors quality demands, we reasoned that safety case style organization of information about the designed technology could be fruitful for validation of the systems usability of a technological system, i.e., also a **systems-usability case** (SUC) could be constructed. It was concluded in addition that a case-based approach may be particularly suitable when the system to be evaluated is unique and comparison to other systems is difficult, as is the case with many complex design products. The method should also support formative evaluation, in which the interest is in steering the system design by connecting information gained in successive evaluations to a set of higher level conceptual requirements. The case would enable an objective reference for evaluations that assume close contact with the design activity. The SUC could also be developed into a living document able to serve as a reference for good human-factors design throughout the design process and during further cycles in the product's service life. We have already tested the SUC approach in creation of innovative design concepts and also in validation of control-room designs for use. Examples are provided in Chapters 4 and 5.

2.3   THE DEVELOPMENTAL APPROACH

Alongside redefining of the unit of analysis, addressed above, we attempt to introduce developmental methodology in human-factors research. It is evident that the practice-theory approach is relevant also with regard to adopting a transformative intention for research. The question is this: To what extent can we treat social practices not only as a unit of analysis but also as a unit of intervention? (Pierce et al., 2013).

The central issue embedded in this matter has to do with the conception of knowledge, especially the relationship between knowledge and action. The practice-theory approach is distinct from mainstream analysis of human conduct in its conception of knowledge. The epistemic assumption of the practice-theory approach is that action is not contrasted against knowledge and that, instead, the foundation of knowledge lies in the interaction between the human and his or her environment, mediated by tools and language. This idea is expressed clearly in American pragmatism, especially in the works of Dewey (e.g. in Dewey, 1999, originally published in 1929). In the cited work, Dewey endorses the idea that knowledge is not certainty about something existing and ready to be discovered; instead, he claims, it is understanding that emerges from interaction with the reality as a result of a **transforming** activity.

2.3.1   FOUNDATIONS FOR A DEVELOPMENTAL RESEARCH APPROACH

The transformative aspect of knowledge that characterizes American pragmatism holds also for CHAT. The epistemic ideas of CHAT were developed further by, among others, Ewald Ilyenkov (1977) and Marx Wartofsky (1979). The theory's concept of mediated action, which articulates the role of artifacts and signs in the interaction of human with environment, also promotes the idea that consciousness and knowledge are found not in the head of the individual but, indeed, in the active interaction of the individual with the environments and its objects. The theory also holds that meaning lies neither in the environment nor in the organism but in the endless mutual transformation between the two (Miettinen, 2006, p. 396, in reference to Ewald Ilyenkov).

With its transformative epistemology, CHAT lays the groundwork for a developmental research approach to human conduct. According to this epistemology, constructing knowledge involves making assumptions as to the object and testing these assumptions in practice that changes the object. The central role of transformative acting in this epistemology is crystallized by Yves Clot, who sees the principle of creating knowledge as "acting, without being able to foresee everything, in order to know" (2010, p. 287). Therefore, in a developmental research approach, the transformation of the object of research is part of the research process itself. This conception might prompt disagreement on the part of those human-factors researchers who see staying detached from the object of research as being the central criterion for the quality of objective knowledge. Such a strong notion of objectivism still has its advocates, but it has also been questioned in science, particularly in the social sciences (Megill, 1997). Allan Megill maintains that subjectivity is a prerequisite for objectivity in the sense that the object is readily created in the personal acting in the world—i.e., in the communicative interaction between the enquirer and the object.

The advantages of the developmental approach with respect to understanding human conduct are elaborated upon by Engeström (2011) in an article explaining some of the principles of developmental work research. One of the most central methodological ideas is labeled the **formative intervention**. To demonstrate the epistemic characteristics of this intervention, he contrasts it against the more traditional design experiment, where the latter refers to a method applied in educational research to facilitate learning and change of practices.

Engeström claims that the fundamental assumption in the traditional design experiment is that researchers know the novel features they want to implement in the activity and also know how to perform the implementation. In other words, the process and outcomes of the interventions are well defined in advance. From this it follows that the intervention actually is a linear process of implementing a change and checking whether the desired outcome is achieved. Opportunities for improvement of the implementation are to be found only in making the learning, or design, process more systematic and controlled.

In contrast to what is described above, the formative intervention stresses the openness of the learning or the design process. It is not clear how the system designed or the new practices will look. Therefore, the solutions must be created by the participants during the intervention. It is additionally assumed that there is resistance to change in the present system or among the relevant professionals, and that this resistance when reflected upon may be extremely important in relation to invention of new solutions. It is also emphasized that the professional subjects of the intervention are active agents in the construction of the solution, which means that they also become the owners of the solution emotionally. The key point is that all this does not necessarily happen spontaneously in a learning session or even in design workshops, even when these features have been aimed at by the researchers. Instead, creation of new solutions and knowledge must be facilitated. But how?

The vehicle for creating a creative learning process is the principle of double stimulation as articulated by Vygotsky (1978, pp. 74-75). That principle states that in a normal structured learning situation (and in a user-centered design workshop), the learning problems or design problems are the focus of activity. This is, of course, correct, and the theory states that these problems constitute the "first stimulus" that requires response by the participants. The clue is that, for the learning or innovation process to be effective, the participants also need a second element to focus on: a tool or concept that steers the creative process. This element is the "second stimulus." It is created by the experimenter or teacher by active offering, or it may be neutrally available in the environment, able to be discovered by the participants. Its function is to promote creation of a solution to the problem. The process of learning and its result in such a situation are not controlled by the experimenter or teacher; instead, they are accorded agency by the actors themselves who create the solutions.

The drawbacks of design experiments and advantages of formative interventions are listed by Engeström in relation to four main points (Engeström, 2011, p. 606. Italics ours):

1. Starting point: In a linear design experiment, the content and the goals of the intervention are known ahead of time. *In the formative intervention, the participants are confronted with the problems of the activity, which they tackle by exploiting external tools, and develop a novel concept that reflects transformation in the activity.*

2. Process: In the linear design experiment, the researchers execute the transformation and resistance is not expected on the participants' part. *In the formative intervention, dialogue is assumed and the principle of double stimulation is exploited to ensure the active agency of the participants.*

3. Outcome: In the linear design experiment, the outcome is a desired change and a tool for replicating it in the same form in other situations and contexts. *In the formative experiment, the outcome is a concept that enables producing the transformation in accordance with the specific needs of the situation and context.*

4. Researcher's role: In the linear design experiment, the researchers control the process. *In the formative intervention, the process is led and owned by the participants.*

The arguments of Engeström for use of formative interventions appear relevant and useful also for improving human-factors design. Analogously to traditional design experiments, the human-centered design approaches that are currently applied tend not to fulfill the criteria of a formative approach. Methodically mastered formative interventions are rare.

2.3.2   THE CORE-TASK DESIGN MODEL

When one considers the appropriation of formative interventions as a method in human-factors design, it is necessary to bear in mind that the human-factors discipline is directly connected with the design of the artifacts of work. It is apparent that engineers may have practices that offer support for formative interventions. Indeed, the design process and the design activity are known to be nonlinear (Lawson, 1980). The French human-factors scientist Pierre Falzon (2008) emphasizes the problem-solving character of design activity and draws attention to the fact that during the design the problem is defined simultaneously with its resolution. This means that via design (e.g., sketching, prototyping, or simulation), the original design problem is understood more and more profoundly and may thereby become reframed. Because the scale and complexity of the object of design are sometimes so great that in the beginning it is practically impossible to comprehend the couplings involved and the related design problems, the original problem needs to be defined over and over again in the course of the design (Savioja, 2014, p. 59).

Falzon (2008) recognizes the epistemic aspect of design activity and concludes that human-factors experts may even have difficulty in adopting spontaneously formative epistemology. He maintains that design and human-factors activities represent very different scientific paradigms. The human-factors discipline (often) relies on an idea of science that stresses rationality, independence, and control, whereas design as an activity is different. There are ingenious design outcomes that are not based on rationality and in the design of which the designers have become highly involved in the usage activity. Design may produce excellent outcomes and at the same time be participative, iterative, and sometimes even chaotic. According to Alain Findeli, design thinking is parallel and holistic and resembles visual comprehension of objects, i.e., it is a kind of "visual intelligence" (Findeli, 2001).

Kari Kuutti (2009) lists issues that are characteristic of the epistemology of design as "visual intelligence": design knowledge is different from science in that it creates knowledge and utilizes knowledge that is local, particular, and timely: the artifact should work in the near future and meet the identified needs of the users. Science aims at general, global, and timeless knowledge. Design knowledge is also only partially explicit, taking the form of specifications, programs, description of modeling methods, etc. A large proportion of knowledge is embedded in ways of designing and, hence, is not explicit and is taken for granted.

It appears that design activity and its epistemology have commonality with the activity taking place in a formative intervention. However, the conceptual elements of the formative intervention that facilitate the innovation process are typically absent from the design process. Design is focused on the specific product as its result but too seldom on a concept that as a result would provide a more generic solution. On the basis of this observation, Turkka Keinonen proposed that product design should be completed via a design process that he labels "remote design." It has features that enable conceptual control of the design activity and generalizable future-oriented solutions (Keinonen, 2007). In this connection, Keinonen also points out that product design has already been largely complemented by the contribution of the end users, in what Keinonen labels "immediate design," but this is restricted to addressing local user needs that are temporary and proximal. The significant role of remote design is to extend the horizon of the design.

An interesting practice-theory-oriented design approach that has much in common with CTD has been presented by Volker Wulf et al. (2011). It is referred to as the design-case study approach. The authors, who adopt the perspective of computer science research, study practices with a transformative intent. Their primary focus is on the design of technical artifacts that should be transformative with regard to a certain problem or need in a specific domain of practice. While the involvement of the professional users is an important element of the design-case study approach, it appears that the role of conceptual means in support of the users' creative input is not articulated in this approach.

We conclude that human-factors experts could take an active role in providing the conceptual tools for structuring a design process, specifically in organizing the collaboration of the actors, designers, and human-factors researchers in a manner facilitating innovations in technology and work. In such an elaborate and dialogue-based design process, the values attached to the development could be taken as an inherent feature of the design process. Indeed, the ethical and moral aspects of design have recently begun to be addressed by human factors-experts as an important area for improvement of the design process, with the aim of its outcomes better reflecting the targeted values and experiences of people (Boy, 2013; Pierce et al., 2013; Wright and McCarthy, 2010; Wulf et al., 2011).

In Core-Task Design, the ethics dimension is deliberately made present. The modeling of the activity system and the use of core-task functions make explicit the values attached to the work activity. By connecting the analysis and design to the meaning or mission of the activity from a societal perspective, the CTD approach does not restrict itself to considering values merely as individual choices and experiences linked to local events. The value perspective is represented in CTD by a modeling method intended for conceptualizing the concept under design. That method, which has been labeled *tools-in-use* (TiU) modeling, is designed to capture the value perspective in CTD. The tools-in-use method will be described in Chapter 4.

CTD also recognizes that development or change does not take place without resistance and contradictions, and it concludes that these need to be made explicit during the design. Core-Task Design also acknowledges the significance of the intentions and agency of individuals and communities for the creativity of design. In addition, it supports the idea that individual and collective agency is a necessary element in a transformative activity.

The Core-Task Design approach is tuned to fulfilling the principles of design outlined above. For realizing the principles, we consider three main design functions to be needed. These are the

understand-to-generalize, **foresee-the-promise**, and **intervene-to-develop** functions. They are depicted in Figure 2.10. The figure also illustrates three states of reality in relation to the activity under consideration: the **actual activity**, **core activity**, and **potential activity**. The design functions are seen as enabling the activity to be viewed from three distinct perspectives. Changing perspective is realized by the design functions, which always are present in design, as they are responsible for its creative power. The prevalence of the functions may vary, however, on the basis of the design process and tasks involved.

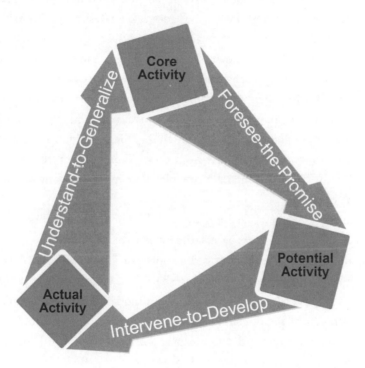

Figure 2.10: The Core-Task Design process, with three design functions that enable transformation of the object of design from concrete actual activity into abstracted core activity, then potential activity, and finally the emerging new actual activity.

2.3.3 THE DESIGN FUNCTIONS IN CORE-TASK DESIGN

We now turn to the three design functions of Core-Task Design, as depicted in Figure 2.10. The main concepts and the corresponding research methods of CTD, introduced earlier in this chapter, are now presented as means actively employed to fulfill the design functions. Several groups of actors collaborate in the activities of the design functions.

The Understand-to-Generalize Function

The first design function is devoted to answering the question of how to generalize from the empirical enquiry about **actual activity**. Data on the current actual work practice are gathered by means of various empirical methods (such as questionnaires, interviews, self-reporting, and observations, which may include a video record, eye-tracking, and audio recordings). In the analysis of the data, the methods of CTD are exploited in such a way as to capture the actual, observable action (timelines of observable actions, focus of attention, errors, self-evaluated mental load, etc.). The analysis of action corresponds to that in most approaches to work analysis, but the focus in this design function is not on the present action as such but on the analysis of the generic element of the present practices. This makes our method unique. We reveal the mechanisms behind the actual action, in which we focus on the orienting mechanisms of activity—i.e., work orientation and habit. User experience too is analyzed. Moving upward from the level of action to the mechanisms of activity, we use conceptual modeling of possibilities for action: we exploit the activity-system, core-task function, situation, and tool-function modeling, which together provide a reference for the analysis of actions. We can, consequently, switch view from description of the actual action to conceiving of the generic mechanism or developmental principles that make the activity what it is, the **core activity** (see Figure 2.10).

Analysis of the complex work of, among others, NPP process operators, ship-bridge personnel, metro traffic controllers, and farmers necessarily involves close collaboration with the sharp-end actors, who participate in research sessions of various sorts during which a rich dataset is created. At the same time, the participants are not restricted to sharp-end actors. We also involve subject-matter experts in the relevant domain, who are invaluable in modeling the activity and identifying the possibilities and constraints of the domain, or the features of a complex automation systems, etc. Involved additionally are managers and safety experts, who may inform of such elements as the organizational routines and safety principles and measures.

The Foresee-the-Promise Function

The second design function is dedicated to answering the question of how to see the promise of new solutions for future work. The analysis here focuses on developing concepts of future **potential activity**. The starting point consists of the functional generalizations of the present work, and the challenge is to project the core content of the work—i.e., the core activity—to optional concepts of new work (see Figure 2.10). A key method in this design function is tools-in-use modeling. The TiU model has three layers: the values of the work, the technology concept, and the user-interface layer. These layers enter into the analysis step by step such that the focus is initially on values of the work and the technology concept; only later are more specific interface solutions considered. The strong role of models and concepts distinguishes this approach from that of typical user-centered design sessions, in which the end user normally considers only the interface layer, which can be made tangible by means of drawings, simulations, or prototypes and about which opinions and other responses are collected. In this, the usual case, the connection to underlying technology concepts or values remains implicit.

The professional actors or users are the agents who provide the main input to TiU modeling. Theirs is the key role in defining the values of work, for which the core-task function models or general descriptions of technological capabilities are used as second stimuli. They also participate in developing and evaluating the solutions with regard to the values in the work. Evaluations may involve comprehensive testing of solution options in, for instance, test or simulation environments. Claims about the designed concepts are developed and evidence sought for testing whether they fulfill the systems-usability criteria. The core contribution of the professional users is an evaluation of the promise of the future technology with regard to outcomes that the individuals and the community of practitioners value. Designers with vendors and production organizations participate actively to create the technology concepts. Doubts and resistance aroused by the proposed concepts are observed, and sessions are organized in which dialogue with designers and, for example, safety engineers can take place. Human-factors experts serve as facilitators who ensure that the design perspectives cover future work and not just technical solutions.

The Intervene-to-Develop Function

The third design function is directed at the question of how to make the change in work happen. In a complex and probably step-wise design process, an intervention may focus on one of the iterations in the process, or the intervention might deal with a mature solution later in the design process. In the intervention function, the perspective is aligned with the new **actual activity** and how to get people to make the concrete change (see Figure 2.10). In the complex work environments in which CTD is meant to be applied, the intervention function may be quite protracted and involve a complex networked organization in which production organizations, vendors, and—in the case of safety-critical work—regulatory bodies are actively involved.

In this function we can identify at least three sub-functions within which CTD methods may be used. The first of these is the evaluation of human–technology systems. This evaluation may serve both design and (regulatory) acceptance of the solution in practice. Systems-usability criteria are used as the basis for formulation of claims to be tested in the evaluation. The second sub-function is development of human competencies. This is considered to be part of the design and is aimed at transforming practices and developing new practices that enable appropriation of the technological solutions designed. The final sub-function is the management of the human-factors design in follow-up on design and operation experience. The fundamental methods of CTD and developmental methodology are included in the toolkit with the aid of which we are able to intervene with the work and support the change. Further tools have been developed for the individual sub-functions of the intervention.

Examples of use of the concepts and methods to carry out the three design functions are provided in Chapters 3, 4, and 5, each of which focuses on one of the three functions, in its turn.

CHAPTER   3

Understanding: How to Generalize from Empirical Enquiry about Actual Work

This chapter deals with the design function that has been given the label "understand-to-generalize." By the notion of understanding, we mean profound knowledge pertaining to the activity being developed in the CTD project. In the understanding function, the activity is thoroughly examined to an extent allowing a first formulation of the core task of the activity and the mechanism that underlie the situationally specific actual activity. As the core task describes the core content and the general objective of the activity, generalized knowledge surrounding the characteristics of the activity must be elicited. Nevertheless, the generalization needs to be grounded in situational details, so analysis of the work system on multiple levels of abstraction is required. This multiple-level analysis means connecting the societal purpose of the activity to the everyday work people carry out. The end result of the analysis, an elaborated description of the core task that covers the situational and the general aspects of the work, is necessary for ensuring that the design efforts do not concentrate on irrelevant details of the current work or possible present problems and "quick fixes" to them.

Understanding the core task of particular target work is challenging for a researcher or a developer who is not an expert in the field in question. The researcher enters the domain by merely exploring the workplace in person and observing the work, interviewing the professionals, familiarizing him- or herself with tools and documents related to the work, etc. Even though material is typically collected in abundance and the researcher slowly starts to build an overall picture of the work, it is still difficult to identify the important generic mechanisms explaining the formation of work from the situational features that have been discovered.

The data collection is conducted on a situational foundation, meaning that researchers observe particular work situations and are able to interview a certain number of employees within the system. Yet the findings (i.e., the habits and the core activity expressed by the core task) should be an abstraction not unnecessarily affected by the current way of conducting the work. The core activity has to do with the general formative principles in the work, not external features of the current actions. The aim with the understand-to-generalize function is to identify the "germ cell" of the activity, the content that is always present in every detail-level action but also identifiable as a principle that must always be fulfilled if the goals for the activity are to be reached. Identifying the core activity, including core task, orientation, and habits, should allow holistic development of the system without unnecessary sub-optimization as might result from operating at the level of current tasks.

In this chapter, we present the methods developed for conceptualizing the core task and habits of an activity. A case study conducted in the nuclear power production context and having to do with bringing emergency operating procedures into use is presented as an example. The case study has been reported upon in its entirety in an article by Savioja et al. (2014) . The description in this chapter concentrates on the methods and the challenge of the understanding function, which is to see the general in the particular.

3.1   THE PRACTICAL PROBLEM IN THE EXAMPLE CASE

This CTD effort was conducted at a Finnish NPP that had already revamped its emergency operating procedures (EOPs). The plant was interested in knowing how well the new EOPs had been adopted by the operating crews and how the process-control work was affected by the adoption of the new tool.

In an NPP context, EOPs constitute an extremely important defence against several threats: They allow for advance planning and thereby for training in the process-control activities to be performed in foreseeable difficult process situations. This planning and training is expected to lessen the task load of the human operators in difficult situations and so diminish the overall probability of humans carrying out erroneous actions.

The problem with EOPs is that they can only be designed for situations that can be thought of in advance. Procedures cannot cover situations that are totally unexpected and therefore surprising, yet the latter are often the most difficult situations to handle and, accordingly, may cause greater risk to the overall safety of the system. For this reason, conducting procedural work is not easy or straightforward. The human operators using EOPs can never be totally certain that the current situation is the one that the current procedure is addressing, yet they must be able to act on the situation with the knowledge they have to hand. In order to resolve this contradiction, the operators must always maintain sensitivity to possible subtle and unexpected changes in the process situation that may be indications of the current procedure not fitting the situation. Also, the human operators must constantly analyze whether the procedure is working correctly or instead there are signs pointing toward a need to shift to a different procedure. It is always possible that the process situation is something other than what it first looks like, and this mismatch may cause the procedure not to work or even to be harmful from the perspective of overall safety goals for the plant. In other words, the usage of EOPs should be "intelligent" (Filippi, 2006). Procedures cannot be merely followed without reflection about the developing situation. Use of procedures should not be blind following of what is prescribed; rather, it should be an active process of constantly both conducting operations effectively and assessing whether the procedure actually suits the particular situation at hand.

All NPP operation can be characterized as procedural work, as procedures exist for several operative tasks and separately for activities in process-disturbance, incident, and accident conditions. The central problem in procedural activity can be defined as that of finding the right balance between stability and flexibility. On one hand, the aim of the procedures is to stabilize activity: provide pre-planned courses of action that human operators can rely on. But, simultaneously, as it is well known that it is impossible to pre-plan all activities in our unpredictable world, room for flexibility should be allowed. Striking the right balance is both a question of concrete procedure design and one of using the procedure in the activity.

The aim of the study taken as an example here was to investigate how the new EOPs had been adopted by the operation crews. In particular, we were interested in whether the crews had struck the right balance between stability and flexibility in using the new procedures. The research question was designed for judging (1) whether intelligent use of procedures existed with the new EOPs and, at the same time, (2) what would be the characteristics of intelligent procedure use in this context. The study followed the CTD process, since another objective was to identify new ways of working with the EOPs that should be implemented in the standard paths of process-control work.

For in-depth understanding of EOP usage, we conducted a study at an NPP training simulator. All of the plant's operating crews participated and utilized the new EOPs in particular simulated accident scenarios.

3.1.1   PARTICULARITIES OF THE PLANT

The nuclear power plant in the case study is a pressurized-water reactor (PWR) consisting of two separate units. The plant dates from the late 1970s, and each unit currently produces close to 500 MW of electrical power. A normal control-room operating crew consists of three operators: a shift supervisor (SS), a reactor operator (RO), and a turbine operator (TO). The responsibilities of the operators are divided such that the RO takes care of the primary circuit: heat generation and cooling. The TO's responsibility is turbine operation and electricity generation. Finally, the SS has a leading role in making crucial operative decisions and supervizing the duties of both RO and TO. In all, 44 operators took part in the study. The participants' operation experience ranged from 1 to 32 years, with the majority of the subjects having around 10 years' experience.

3.1.2   EMERGENCY OPERATING PROCEDURES USED AT THE PLANT

The case-study NPP had recently renewed its EOPs to follow flowchart style. A flowchart EOP (see Figure 3.1 for an example) is conceptualized with lines and question boxes. The operator enters a page along a certain line, which leads to a question box. If the question in the box is answered "yes," the line downward from the box gets followed. If the answer is "no," the line running to the side of the box is to be followed. In addition, the EOP page states the actions that are connected to a certain line or box. A page may also feature questions that must be continuously considered and some other elements.

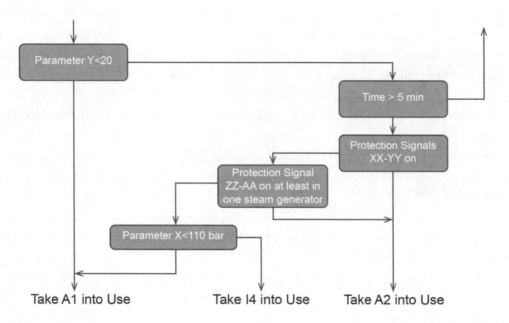

Figure 3.1: A flowchart-type procedure design is composed of question boxes, lines leading from box to box, and action commands.

3.1.3   A SIMULATED ACCIDENT SCENARIO

A design basis accident, a loss-of-coolant accident (LOCA), was utilized as a research situation. The specific LOCA was mid-sized, which at this plant means that the reactor and turbine scrams were automatically actuated, containment isolation was completed, and action of safety-injection water systems was initiated by the automatic system. Also, diesel generators were started up, to assure an energy supply for safety systems. In this specific scenario, there was one additional simulated failure in the safety systems: because a certain plant protection signal did not function correctly, containment isolation was not completed automatically.

The operators' tasks in this type of scenario consist mainly of double-checking and assuring that all automatic safety systems are functioning as required and of further identification of the situation (e.g., the leak's locale).

3.2   CORE-TASK DESIGN METHODS IN THE UNDERSTAND-TO-GENERALIZE FUNCTION

The individual methods utilized in the understanding function are presented in the following discussion.

3.2.1   IDENTIFICATION OF CORE-TASK FUNCTIONS

In this study, the template for the core-task functions model presented in Chapter 2 was populated with characteristics of NPP operation work. The dynamism, complexity, and uncertainty features of the NPP process were explicated with the aid of domain experts. The model formulated for the environmental possibilities and constraints is presented below (as Figure 3.2).

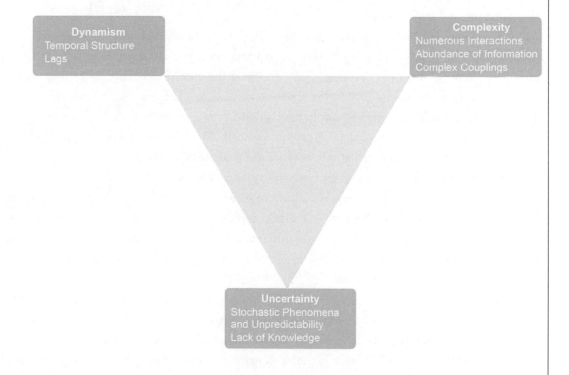

Figure 3.2: The environmental possibilities and the constraints to NPP operation.

The human resources that control-room operators need for carrying out the work successfully were contextualized as core-task functions (CTFs) (see also Figure 3.3). Before presentation of the CTFs, it must be noted that, although they are presented here as-is, their formulation is of an iterative nature, taking place throughout the CTD process. What is presented here is the formulation we ended up with at the end of the study, representing our current understanding of the essential, core content of the NPP operators' work.

To determine the CTFs for the NPP domain, we need to see what kinds of human activity the environmental possibilities and constraints of the particular domain require. The subsections below present what kinds of skills, knowledge, and reflective resources are needed for responding appropriately to the environmental possibilities of and constraints within the NPP process presented above (in Figure 3.2).

Skill-Related Core-Task Functions in NPP Process-Control Work

We have labeled the pragmatic human resources as skills. The core-task functions related to skills indicate how humans should act in order to respond appropriately to the environmental possibilities and constraints of the domain.

Readiness to act as a core-task function means that the continuously ongoing process phenomena must be acted on in a timely manner and that sufficient certainty about what is the right thing to do must be achieved quite rapidly by the operating crew. This entails the crew grasping the critical features of the complexity of the situation (see below). It is understandable that people in safety-critical domains may be hesitant to take action, because of the irreversible consequences that many actions have (there is no "undo" in process control). But, as a situation develops, the operating crews must be ready to perform actions in order to take control of the situation. A certain amount of courage that reflects appropriate professional confidence is demanded of the operating crew.

For mastering complexity, it is important to focus the actions on the most critical aspects of the process. This is important because in a vast, complex system, less significant details too may be manifested in the situation while time always remains limited. So action should not be wasted on issues of no importance. The skill related to mastery of complexity is identified as **ability to focus on the critical aspects of the process**.

Sometimes actions are needed even though the picture of the information on the situation is still incomplete or contains uncertainties. This may, in fact, be the case almost always. In this kind of situation, it is important to take action, test alternatives, and thereby create more information pertaining to the situation. We refer to the skills needed to master uncertainty as **testing and narrowing down the possibilities**.

Knowing-Related Core-Task Functions in NPP Process-Control Work

Knowing refers to the epistemic resources people have in complex work. These resources are crucial in a domain that represents a specialist field. From the standpoint of knowing, it is important to have a very profound understanding of the principles of the process behavior, the types of interaction that occur in the system, and what the dynamic phenomena are that take place in the various kinds of process situations.

For mastery of dynamism from the angle of knowing, we emphasize understanding of the temporal features of the process phenomena, such as how rapidly events evolve or the existence of long time lags. As a central operating task encompasses connecting the right procedure to the situation, it is important to be sensitive to the first indications of the process status changing. Accordingly, we have labeled the knowing involved in mastering dynamism as **perceiving weak signals and anticipating**.

Knowing for mastery of complexity means that human operators must know and understand how the details make up the whole complex process. It is important to see how quite different sub-processes are brought together to serve the overall functions of the process. Operators must be able also to explain these issues in their own words and on this basis to develop accurate process feel. The knowing-related demand for mastering complexity we refer to as **concept-mastery and comprehending of wholes**.

Uncertainty is a general characteristic of the NPP process. Not all phenomena can be predicted and empirically proved. Therefore, epistemically, the human operators must be able to always interpret process information, create and accumulate knowledge by means of their own experience of the process, and possibly reorient themselves if it seems that a previous interpretation does not work anymore. The knowing demanded for mastering uncertainty has been labeled as **interpreting and reorienting**.

Collaboration- and Reflection-Related Core-Task Functions in NPP Process-Control Cork

The heuristic resources in work we have denoted as collaboration and reflection. With these words, we emphasize the role of communication in complex work. People need to formulate communications with each other and with themselves (the latter through reflection) in order to manage the demanding work. Communication is a way of creating new knowledge, and—as are all other human resources—it is needed for management of the possibilities and constraints created by the environment.

Collaboration and reflection for mastery of dynamism refers to the capability of the operators to defend against the tendency toward being "captured" by the ongoing situation and developing tunnel vision with respect to it. An information-intensive event may also readily exhaust the capability of an operator to reason about the situation. **Optimal sharing of efforts** is desired of all operators but is a particular responsibility of the shift supervisor when he or she notices potential for overload or inability to proceed properly in the task.

Collaboration and reflection for mastering complexity points to the fact that the operative situations in the NPP always require well-coordinated independent and joint actions. The appropriateness and fluency of joint actions assume conscious creation of shared awareness of the situation and agreement on the situational goals.

Collaboration and reflection for mastery of uncertainty highlights the epistemic aspect of collaboration. Operators should be able and willing to make their reasoning explicit to fellow operators and, in turn, to listen to the others' opinions and reasoning. Such a form of open communication enables perspectives to be contrasted and affords joint construction of knowledge of phenomena and situations that have not been encountered before. In short, there needs to be dialogue for creating knowledge with both self and others.

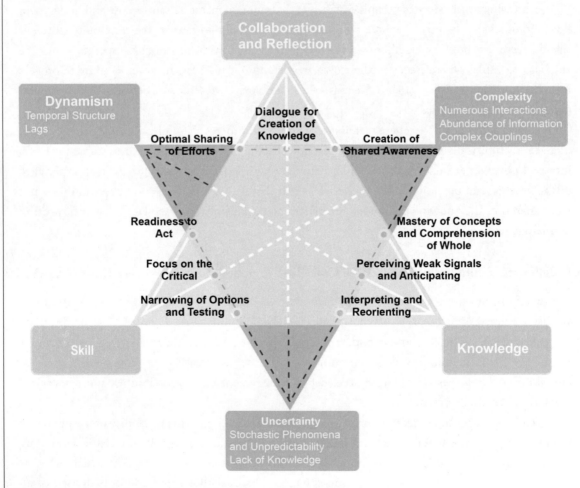

Figure 3.3: Core-task functions in NPP process-control work.

3.2.2   DESIGN AND ANALYSIS OF THE SIMULATED SCENARIO (FUNCTIONAL SITUATION MODELING)

The next CTD method presented here deals with analysis of the situational aspects of NPP operation work, especially how the general core-task demands are represented in the particular situations that are being studied. Hence, we present the situation-analysis method that is used for creating functional situation models.

Creating research situations, which in our case study were simulated accident scenarios, is an essential step in any empirical research. As the aim of the understanding function in CTD is to dissect the central aspects of the activity being developed, it is crucial that the right kinds of research situations be created and their representativeness in relation to the core task be analyzed. For this purpose—i.e., to understand the research situations from a general perspective—we have created the functional situation modeling technique. It also serves as a situational task-analysis method.

In general, task analysis is aimed at describing what people must do to accomplish a particular goal. Typically, task analysis addresses particular situations on the level of actions and answers the question of what must be done in which situation (consider, for example, hierarchical task modeling, HTA (Stanton, 2006; Vicente, 1999). Hence, a connection between the situational actions and the general demands of the work is not made. However, this connection is important, because it explicates the meaning of the individual actions from the standpoint of the general objective of the work. The task model is used as a reference when one is analyzing the observed activity of the actual operating crews. If the analysis is aimed at understanding how these crews are able to attend to the general objectives of the work while simultaneously carrying out the situationally important actions, the reference model should address this aspect also.

The main inspiration for the FSM approach is Rasmussen's (1986) control-domain modeling, the abstraction hierarchy (AH). The AH represents the system controlled and its environment at multiple levels of means–end abstractions. This approach is fundamentally different from HTA, in which the relationship between subsequent levels is part-to-whole. In an abstraction hierarchy, each level constitutes a qualitatively different abstraction of the system. In AH-based work, the viewpoint is specifically aligned with the constraints governing the functioning of the system. However, the AH is a general model of the domain. For the purpose of understanding the demands of activity in particular situations, specific models of situations are needed.

FSM combines two perspectives on the situation being modeled: a task-based view and a function-based view. The two together define a two-dimensional space in which the most important operator actions and process phenomena are mapped for the purpose of understanding both operating performance and the ways of taking the general objective into account in the performance (i.e., habit).

The Task-Based View of the Situation

The task-based perspective is the most obvious angle from which to analyze the operating activity. In the associated view, the scenario is divided roughly into phases, in each of which the operating actions have a specific goal. In the example FSM (Figure 3.4), the tasks are labeled in accordance with the goals of the individual phases in the scenario: detection, mitigation of effect, diagnosis, and stabilizing of the process state.

Although a distinction is made among the goals, it must be acknowledged that in real-world activity all the goals are somehow present simultaneously. But for the purpose of making sense of the process situation, the distinction is nevertheless made in FSM. Also, in different circumstances, these phases might have different goals, in which case different labels for the phases should be utilized.

Detection

In the model, the detection phase denotes that the crew identify some process events requiring operator actions. The process information presented to the operators typically consists of alarm information and notifications. Simultaneously, monitoring of all process information is conducted by the crew.

In the model depicted here (in Figure 3.4), the detection phase is concerned with the information that is available to the operators for understanding of deviations in the process. It is also important to identify and explicate the initial event(s). The most important alarms informing the operators are included in the model. The implications of the initial event for the process state are depicted on parameter and overall process level.

Mitigation of the effect

The line between mitigation and detection is not always distinct, since the operating activity actually constitutes a continuous cycle of monitoring and acting. Therefore, the exact point in time when the mitigation phase "starts" is not so important, but we do want to draw the distinction that some operation actions are tuned more toward mitigating the situation than to perceiving information about the situation. It is also typical that automatic functions handle some of the actions in this phase. In this case, important operator actions involve confirming successful execution of the automatic functions. In the mitigation phase in the model, the operating actions that mitigate the process situation are mapped under the specific process information items and initial events of the detection phase to which they are connected.

Diagnosis

Since the ultimate operating goal in an accident situation is to bring the process into a safe, stable state, diagnosis-related actions are required from the operating crew. It is important to recognize what the process situation is, for identification of the required actions. In the diagnosis phase, these actions are depicted in the model under the specific parameters within the detection phase that they are related to.

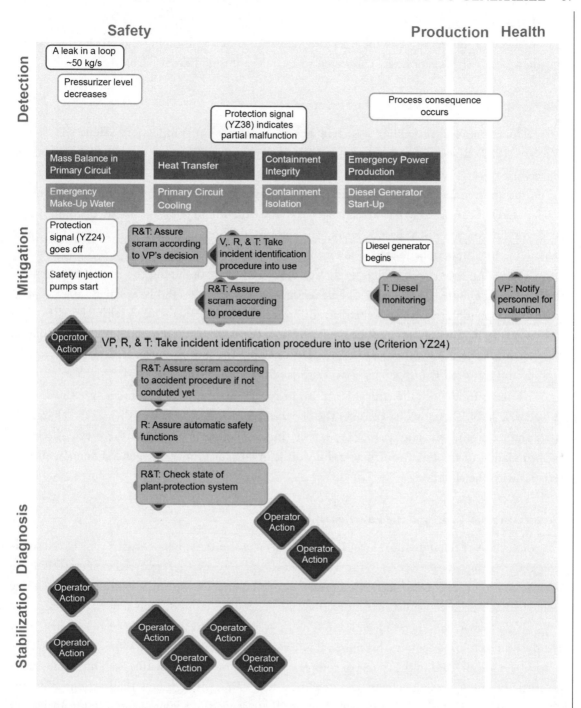

Figure 3.4: The functional situation model for our "loss-of-coolant" case.

Stabilization

The stabilization phase refers to the operating activities aimed at bringing the process into a safe and stable state. These actions are connected to the relevant initial events also.

The Function-Oriented View of the Situation

A well-functioning socio-technical system has the objectives of production, safety, and health (Vicente, 1999). These objectives form the basis of the function-oriented view in FSM (the three "lanes" in Figure 3.4).

The most important items in the functional view are the critical functions (e.g., Norros, 2004, p. 111) of the process that are endangered in the situation in question. These functions might be, depending on the initial events, related to safety, production, or health. Typically in a complex situation, critical functions related to all of these objectives are endangered.

Operating activity, on a high level, is oriented toward maintaining the critical functions of the process. Therefore, the operator actions required in the situation can be collated under general means of responding to the endangerment of critical functions. This is depicted in FSM by presenting a specific function level in the model, of "functional means to respond." This level connects the individual operating actions to the critical functions. The link from the critical-function level upward and from individual actions downward is of the type means–end.

If one is to identify the critical functions in a situation, it is importan to analyze the domain at a general level. Therefore, we consider the domain from the perspective of the general characteristics and determine the core task of the activity in the manner presented in the previous section. In formulation of the functional view in FSM, it is important to map the general domain characteristics with the situation.

Connecting the Task- and the Function-Based View

Via connection of the individual-level actions of the crew and the function-based view of the situation, the meaning of each action in the wider context of the scenario is rendered explicit. This is the most important aspect of a functional situation model: it enables the analysis of operating activity from the habit perspective because it describes the general meaning of each action.

If and when the operating crew are tuned toward the critical functions of the domain, they are always taken into account. This means that the crew as a unit follows how the critical functions behave and are affected in the course of complex process-control activity. This is an important characteristic of safe operating activity: the crew must fully think through how their actions affect the process and be present in the particular situation. These aspects of activity belong to the analysis of crew habits. They are not addressed by typical performance analysis, based as it is on conventional task-analysis methods.

3.2.3   SEMIOTIC ANALYSIS OF HABITS

The third method under the understanding function that is aimed at defining the core activity deals with analyzing observed crew activity and identifying the mechanisms that create continuity to activity over various situations.

Data Collection and Initial Analysis

The empirical collection of data on EOP usage was carried out through observation of actual crew activities in a particular accident situation, the LOCA scenario. The simulator-based study was conducted in conjunction with the operating crews' yearly training. Also, each individual operator was interviewed via the work-orientation interview method.

The operating activity of each crew in the simulated accident scenario was observed both on-line and via recordings. The recordings were in audio, video, and simulator-log format: each operator wore a head-mounted camera, which enabled analysis of direction of gaze and communications. In addition, there were video cameras for a wider view and audio recorders registering operating activity. The process events and all operations were recorded in simulator logs.

The initial analysis and organization of the data involved selecting the most relevant episodes of activity and transcribing them into spreadsheets in which the courses of action of each crew were depicted on detail level. The selection of relevant episodes was based on the model generated in the FSM and also on the research questions. The spreadsheet included process operations, verbal communications, movements (people's position in the control room), and directions of gaze for each crew and each individual crew member.

This initial analysis provides the description of the actual activity: We were able to determine what each crew did in the relevant episode. But the important question in the study was whether the operating crews were able to reach the general goals of the activity, meet the core-task demands, when utilizing the new EOPs. For an answer to this question, it is not enough to understand *what* was done in the situation; also the question of *how* the actions were conducted needs to be answered. Therefore, we proceeded to the next phase in the analysis, the identification of habits.

Identification of Habits

As the aim was to study EOP usage on a general level and reveal the orienting mechanisms behind the actual situation-specific actions, further data analysis was conducted, using the semiotic concept of habit. This analysis is referred to as semiotic analysis of habits, or "habit analysis" for short. It deals with understanding how people take the features of the environment into account in their actions and what meaning they connect to their actions.

The theoretical roots of habit analysis lie in the American philosophical tradition of pragmatism, in which habit is the concept that has been proposed to express the way an organism is organized to respond to the changing and unexpected features of the environment. Peirce and Dewey were among the philosophers who saw habit as a fundamental principle of human thinking and action (Dewey, 2002; Peirce, 1998e): human actors connect themselves to the possibilities of the environment by continuous action–perception cycles, during which assumptions about the environment are formed, outcomes of actions are observed, and a meaningful relationship with the environment is built. Relatively stable anticipatory schemes, habits, emerge when an appropriate response to and interpretation of the environment is reached. Habit repeats because of its meaning. According to Peirce's theory, habit is a triadic element, with three components (as discussed in "Orientation and Habit." Section 2.2.3): *sign*, *interpretant*, and *object*. The three components are interconnected as depicted in Figure 3.5 below.

The interpretant is the element of habit that is directly observable in the behavior of the actor. A person's manner of acting is driven by interpretation of the signs in the environment. The term "sign" refers to any perceivable element or feature of the environment, such as a technology-mediated sound or a visual attribute, or even a deed (e.g., communication or movement) of another person. The object reveals the target or idea to which the sign refers via the interpreting behavior. In other words, the way the crew act on the basis of particular signs reveals what they consider the situation to demand from them.

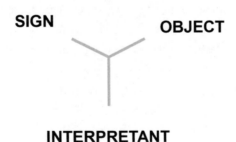

Figure 3.5: The semiotic structure of habit (Peirce, 1958).

Identification of habits was conducted for each episode and for each crew separately. In the habit analysis, we looked at the perception–action cycles in the episode of interest and focused first on what people did—i.e., on the deeds as interpretants. In this step, the key operations (verbalizations, acts, movements, etc.) of each crew member in the episode were written out in textual form (this was actually already done in the initial data manipulation, described in the previous section). The next step was to look at the moments immediately prior to the deed and identify the signs on the basis of which the particular operations were carried out. Among the signs, which varied case-specifically, were previous actions, process information, information in the EOP, sounds, and communications. It was not always obvious what sign had triggered the interpretation process, because human action is continuous, but in most cases we were able to come to a conclusion as to what constituted the sign on a suitable level of abstraction. In the final step, we deduced the object in the habit by analytically comparing the interpretant, the sign, and the demands of the process situation described in the model generated in FSM.

As this analysis of perception–action cycles was carried out for the entire dataset, we identified noticeable variance in the crews' behaviors. We identified critical process-control tasks in which variation between crews was obvious: information usage, situation identification, dealing with automation, decision-making, communication, and leadership. All crews conducted these process-control tasks in compliance with the procedure, but the micro level of the behavior, the ways of conducting the tasks—i.e., the habits of information usage, habits of situation identification, habits of dealing with automation, habits of decision-making, habits of communication, and habits of leadership—were internally different. Sometimes crews acted on the basis of different signs, sometimes the same signs were interpreted differently, and so on. This finding leads to the conclusion that different crews directed their activity toward different objects.

Classifying and Grading of Habits

The next task in the analysis was to see what the significance of the variance within the habits was. We started by analyzing similarities and differences qualitatively. In nearly all habits (habits of decision-making, identification of the situation, etc.), we identified classes that fit the classes "interpretative," "confirmative," and "reactive" as defined above on the basis of the Peircean theory, for differences in the creative strength of habits (see Chapter 2 and Norros, 2004): An interpretative habit is such that behaviors can be identified that point in the direction of expressing interest in the present situation and encouraging one's own interpretation of situational demands, questioning the observed phenomena, building expectations of future events, and hence expressing creation of knowledge in action. Nearly an opposite type of habit is the reactive habit. A reactive habit is such that it reflects immediate reaction and passivity in the sense of lack of building expectations pertaining to the situation. No indications of personal interpretations and reflections are identified in the data. A weakness of reactive habit is that it is able only to react to situations; there are no anticipatory aspects, and there is minimal knowledge creation. In a confirmative habit, a necessary counterpart to the sign already exists and the connection is refreshed in action. The particularities of the present situation are not at the focus of attention. Confirmative habit can be described as taking the situation for granted, acting in a predefined way, and overemphasizing rules and procedures. In a confirmative habit, unlike an interpretative habit, repetition does not include reflection. The reflective repetition gives adaptive potential to the interpretative habit. We utilized these predefined labels of habit types as a frame for analysis, but the qualitative characteristics of each class were grounded in the data from observations.

The background assumption in using this specific internal typology of habits is that interpretiveness in operation habits may be a mechanism of producing resilience in the system. For example, an alarm as a sign might be interpreted by seeking other process indications confirming that particular alarm, an interpretative habit, which is a resilience-producing habit of action because it is oriented to the process information and making thorough sense of the situation, whereas the same alarm could be interpreted instead by conducting exactly and only the action the alarm points to. The kind of habit represented by reacting to alarms can be argued to have less capacity to produce system-level resilience because it takes the alarm information provided for granted and does not aim at contextual interpretation of the situation.

An example of the results of habit analysis is presented below (in Figure 3.6). It has to do with habits of information usage. The interpretant—the action that has been observed in the behavior of each crew—is "conducting the scram." The interpretant was the same for all crews. Each one handled the scram as was necessary in the situation, but the crews differed in the signs on whose basis the scram was conducted. Some crews utilized redundant and diverse information in order to validate properly the need for scramming. This was concluded to be an interpretative habit because it shows in-depth interest in the actual situation. Some crews utilized only redundant information—for example, the same information but from different systems. This behavior indicated a confirmative habit in which double-checking is performed more as a rule than as a truly necessary act in the given situation. The crews who used only a single piece of information were concluded to have a reactive habit.

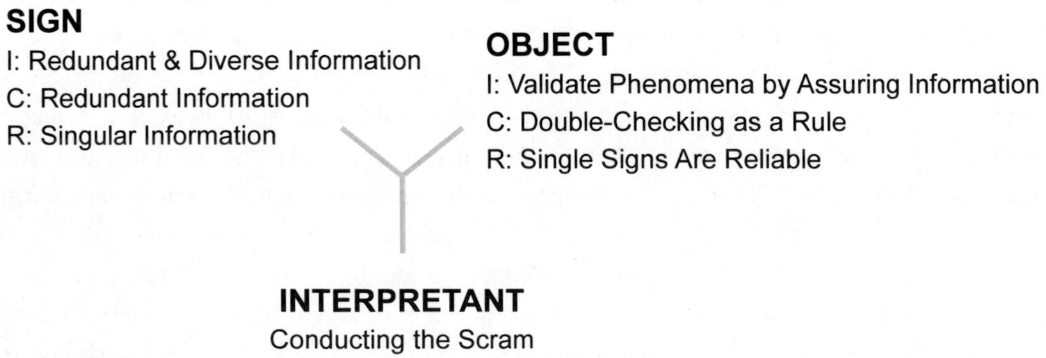

SIGN
I: Redundant & Diverse Information
C: Redundant Information
R: Singular Information

OBJECT
I: Validate Phenomena by Assuring Information
C: Double-Checking as a Rule
R: Single Signs Are Reliable

INTERPRETANT
Conducting the Scram

Figure 3.6: Crew habits related to information usage.

3.3   FINDINGS IN THE STUDY: DIFFERENT WAYS OF USING PROCEDURES

The practical problem in the study surrounded the usage and adaptation of the new EOPs. We needed to find out how well the new EOPs function for their objective of supporting the work of NPP process operators—in other words, fulfillment of the core task of the NPP operating work.

By analyzing the habits of all crews in the selected episodes, we were able to see that in roughly 32% of the episodes analyzed, crews were able to work in a manner in which a connection to the general objectives of the work was established during carrying out of the situationally important actions; i.e., the crews were able to work in an interpretative way. Confirmative habits were the most prevalent, with a share of about 41%, and reactive habits' share was 27%. This result indicates that the new EOPs do not in themselves hinder good work habits, but, if one wishes to increase the share of interpretative habits, it would be necessary that operators be challenged (e.g., in training) to reflect on their ways of acting and to be made aware of the difference between the confirmative and the interpretative habits.

An even more significant practical finding of the study was linked to the qualitative descriptions of the individual kinds of habits in the identified process-control tasks. By carefully analyzing the habits of the crews, we were able to pinpoint differences that are not obvious if the analysis is conducted on the level of actions. Accordingly, it was possible to describe different habits in, for instance, dealing with automation (see Table 3.1). These descriptions are important because they describe the variance in crew habits within following of procedure. It may often be considered enough for the operating crew to follow set procedures in a given situation; however, the analysis we conducted shows that procedure-following may encompass different kinds of habits, some of which are more advantageous than others for the overall safety of production.

Table 3.1: Description of the types of habits of dealing with automation in the LOCA scenario	
Dealing with automation	
Interpretative	The human assures automatic functions. Responsibility is shared between humans and automation
Confirmative	Automatic functioning is observed but not acted upon. There is reliance on predefined roles of human and automation
Reactive	Automation information is taken for granted. There is total reliance on automation

3.3.1   CONCLUSIONS ON THE UNDERSTAND-GENERALIZE CORE-TASK DESIGN FUNCTION

Here we have looked at understanding the empirical reality of the activity that is under development. The aim of the entire CTD process is to avoid the well-known pitfalls of the task–artifact cycle, meaning that the new solutions should not be restricted by current ways of conducting the work. Nevertheless, as the best way to find out about the work is to study it as it now takes place in reality, new ways of analyzing the data are desperately needed. For this purpose, we have developed analysis methods that do not generalize on a statistical basis. Instead, the methods presented in this chapter are based on abstracting and finding the overarching principles governing the whole activity. Through this approach, the new solutions will be developed in a manner grounded in this abstraction, which we call the core activity.

We have demonstrated three central methods for defining the core activity: (1) Core-task modeling for definition of the objectives of work and the core-task functions; (2) functional situation modeling; and (3) semiotic habit analysis. Each of these methods serves the purposes of abstracting empirical findings, but each addresses the problem from a slightly different perspective. By means of these methods, one can delineate the core content and mechanisms of the activity.

The core-task modeling method, designed for identifying the objectives and the core-task functions of a particular activity, is a starting point of the understanding function. In this analysis, the activity system and the environment-generated possibilities and constraints specific to the domain are first analyzed (this is possible with the aid of subject-matter experts). This step produces a description of the dynamism, complexity, and uncertainty (DCU) features of the domain. In the next phase, the human resources—skills, knowledge, and reflection—are mapped to the DCU characteristics. The end result of the analysis, a conceptualization of the core-task functions, is formulated via analytical comparison of the DCU characteristics of the domain with the human resources. The core-task functions are an abstraction of the activity. They are principles governing the work overall, but they can also be identified in the real-world actions observable in people's activity taking place on a daily basis.

Functional situation modeling produces a reference that enables investigating operating activity from the perspective of connecting situational actions to the general objectives of the activity. This is possible because in a model created in FSM the operations required of the operating crew in the particular situation are connected to the general objectives of the activity and also to the general means of reaching the objectives. Therefore, FSM provides a generalization of a situation and thereby serves the purpose of abstracting activity.

Semiotic analysis of habits is a method suitable for analyzing empirically observed activity. In this analysis, the object of observation is how people take information provided by the environment into account in their actions. From this information, it is possible to infer the extent to which the individuals are able to connect the actions to the overall purposes of the activity. The ways of acting, the habits, can be graded by their interpretativeness. In our studies, we found the three classes interpretative, confirmative, and reactive to be of great use. The analysis of habits serves the purpose of abstraction by shifting the focus from individual actions to the generic mechanism underlying the actions.

The understand-to-generalize function grounds the other functions of CTD against the general core characteristics of the activity being developed. This generalization is not arbitrary. It is based on the observed real activity and therefore provides ecologically valid information to inform development of the activity toward meeting its goals. In utilizing the methods described in this chapter, the other design functions too become active. For example, intervention to develop is present when professionals are engaged in reflection on their core task, in that it allows them to see their work from a different perspective, which is often the starting point for change. Similarly, foreseeing the promise is present in the semiotic analysis of habits if the current systems are being scrutinized for their potential to support interpretativeness in acting. Nevertheless, the main focus of the methods presented in this chapter is on reaching the goal of the understand-to-generalize function, which is to understand the general mechanisms governing the activity in the particular research situations.

CHAPTER 4

Foreseeing: How to Uncover the Promise of Solutions for Future Work

A professional can recognize and appreciate when he or she is using a well-functioning tool. However, in the development phase, acknowledging core-task-orientation and nurturing the most promising features of the designed tools is not readily actualized. This chapter focuses on the methods of follow-through in the design process to foresee the potential usefulness—that is, the promise of the design solutions for future work.

We demonstrate CTD's foresee-the-potential function through a case study of evaluation of an innovative human–system interface (HSI) concept in the context of NPP turbine-side process control. The concept evaluated, Functional Integrated Treatments for Novative Ecological Support System (FITNESS for short), was originally developed at Électricité de France (EDF), with the aim being its use in the design of an HSI for control rooms corresponding to the N4 reactor type. In the end, however, the FITNESS concept was never deployed in real use (perhaps because it represented an interface regime very different from those conventional in the field of NPP operation). Nonetheless and perhaps for that very reason, this novel HSI concept provides an interesting case for study of the promise that it still may offer for the process-control work.

This case study exemplifies CTD methods: the concept of systems usability, the systems-usability case, and tools-in-use modeling.

4.1 THE PRACTICAL PROBLEM IN THE EXAMPLE CASE

Obviously, operation of an NPP is very safety-critical and demands highly trained personnel to carry out the process control. The human–system interfaces used for monitoring and control of the process also have high safety demands and strict standards to be followed. Only well-approved solutions can be accepted in actual operation. Therefore, the design, implementation, and adoption of novel interface technologies and operator support systems in an NPP control-room environment involve a challenging and time-consuming process. It can be said that the NPP field takes an extremely conservative approach to interface technologies if compared to almost any other industry with safety-critical operation. The safety and efficiency of the interface solutions are nearly always prioritized over innovativeness and design explorations.

The main tasks of the operating crew at a nuclear power station are to monitor and control the processes related to the power production and to maintain nuclear safety. Monitoring and control operations have been traditionally carried out with a hard-wired analog HSI, but a change-over from analog to digital technologies is now in progress. Generally, digitalization of the control-room interfaces is expected to bring many advantages, such as more efficient information processing and more intuitively graspable graphical forms of presentation. These should better support operators in their work.

4.1.1   PARTICULARITIES OF THE CASE STUDY

The study was carried out within the Euratom-funded MMOtion project in 2010. The central objective of MMOtion was to analyze current and future situations associated with man–machine–organization (MMO) processes and the related safety issues in the nuclear power sector, then, proceeding from this analysis, define, elaborate, and propose a detailed European research roadmap applicable for the next decade but with particular focus on 2011–2015 (MMOTION, 2011). In addition, a small-scale pilot exercise (examining the feasibility of addressing the roadmap topics) was carried out alongside the roadmap's preparation (Norros et al., 2011). The focus of the pilot was on demonstrating methodology to support the human-factors evaluation of an innovative technical concept (i.e., control-room HSI).

The "innovative technical concept" selected for evaluation was the FITNESS system, a development simulator platform located at EDF's SEPTEN site in Villeurbanne, France. It simulates a 1300 MW pressurized-water reactor with an innovative computerized human–system interface concept. The FITNESS HSI concept incorporates three specific innovations to improve the monitoring and control of the processes: (1) functional structuration/presentation of the process; (2) aggregated/operation-context-sensitive alarms; and (3) a proposal of optimal automation level. The FITNESS HSI covers only parts of the turbine (secondary) side of the NPP and allows operations to be performed on these. The level of automation of the FITNESS computerized procedure system can be adjusted in real time, if this is desired, to test the various automation concepts. More detailed description of the FITNESS approach can be found in the work of O'Hara et al. (2003).

Even though the FITNESS system has an advanced material form—a functioning human–system interface connected to the corresponding simulator platform—it can still be considered to represent the concept phase of development if compared to any final control-room product in NPP context. The system is far from an integrated design solution that could be tested as a functioning system embedded in its context of use, as part of a new concept of operation. Instead, FITNESS as an alternative future HSI concept enables consideration and analysis of diverse technological options and their promise for future concepts of operation. The concept evaluation should serve an innovative function and seek design feedback while avoiding an overly conservative approach or the aim of gaining a stamp of the proposed solution's acceptability from the point of view of the end users.

To demonstrate the methodology and to test the promise of the FITNESS concept, evaluation was carried out at the SEPTEN site in April 2010. In total, four operators participated in the evaluation study. All operators were licensed NPP turbine operators, of whom two were Finnish and two were French. The evaluation activities were spread over three days thus: on the first day, the operators were introduced to and trained to operate the FITNESS system; on the second day, five scenario runs were completed by means of the FITNESS system; and facilitated focus-group discussion was held on the third day for a summary of the operators' experiences of the FITNESS system (see Table 4.1).

Table 4.1: Organization of the FITNESS evaluation study

Day 1: Training	Day 2: Scenario runs	Day 3: Focus group
Presentation of the goals of the design experiment	**Theme I: Functional information presentation and FITNESS mode**	**Focus group** on the theme Operators' experience of the potential of the FITNESS system'
Presentation of the principles of the FITNESS simulator and HSI functions	*Scenario 1*: Starting of the conditioning of feed-water systems. FITNESS mode	Visions of the future: HSI in future plants
Free exploration of the FITNESS simulator and HSI functions	**Theme II: Synthesis of plant state and alarms**	**Closing discussion** of the FITNESS evaluation
Closing discussion of the training	*Scenario 4*: Monitoring of the plant at 50% power with leakage in the HP heater. FITNESS mode	
	Scenario 3: Conditioning of the steam lines with leakage in the HP heater. FITNESS mode	
	Theme III: Functional information presen-tation and different operation modes	
	Scenario 1 in procedure mode	
	Scenario 1 in sequence mode	

A systems-usability-case-based method (Norros et al., 2011) was utilized in the preparation, analysis, and documentation of the FITNESS evaluation study. In the SUC process, claims about the usability of the FITNESS concept were specified with the aim of testing how well the product fulfills the human-factors quality demands (that is, systems-usability demands) and how promising the operators experience the proposed concept (design solutions) as being. Iterating evaluation over time while documenting the results in the usability case enables monitoring of systems-usability metrics over time; thereby, the maturation of design can be effectively steered toward the set aims.

4.2 CORE-TASK DESIGN METHODS IN THE FORESEE-THE-PROMISE FUNCTION

The individual Core-Task Design methods utilized in the foresight function are presented below.

4.2.1 THE SYSTEMS-USABILITY EVALUATION FRAME

Tools have a **mediating** role in human activity (Kaptelinin and Nardi, 2012). In the context of process control, this means that the relationship between the subject (the human operator(s)) and the object (the controlled process being acted upon) is mediated by tools and instruments: automation and the control room's human–system interfaces. From the control-room evaluation perspective, good-quality tools, human–system interfaces with good usability, should present the controlled process to the operators in a way that enables appropriate acting on the process. Another aspect of the mediating role of tools is the distinction among the three distinct functions of tools in an activity: the instrumental, psychological, and communicative (see Chapter 2). From the evaluation standpoint, all three tool functions should be considered, and, to achieve good quality—i.e., be a usable system—the tool should fulfill the demands of all three of these functions.

Another relevant perspective for considering the purpose of tools in an activity is **object-orientedness**. According to this principle, the human activity is always directed to the parts of the environment that provide opportunities to maintain and develop human existence. The material (or conceptual) entity toward which the activity is directed forms the object of activity. In process-control work, the automation and its HSIs are used as a tool to control the process (in this specific case, the nuclear power production process) so as to reach the end (here, produce electricity), which is also considered the object of the activity. For successful process-control activity, it is necessary that operators take into account the actual and real possibilities and constraints of the nuclear domain (partly dictated already by the process design) relative to fulfilling the objectives of the activity. In HSI evaluation, this understanding of the object of the activity and the conditional core task (i.e., the main content of the work at hand) can be gained through the functional modeling approach presented in Chapters 2 and 3. The detailing of the core-task functions provides knowledge about what specifically are the features of the object (the dynamism, complexity, and uncertainty features of the object) that the tool is supposed to mediate in order for the operators (by utilizing skill, knowledge, and collaboration and reflection) to fulfill their core task of successfully controlling the process. The object of activity is analyzed to provide contextual characterisation of the tool functions in the relevant work activity. The analysis also compasses the core-task functions that represent the contextually meaningful content of the work, thus providing the basis for identifying appropriateness of activity also from the perspective of tools.

Observing and analyzing the actual work activity is essential when one conducts evaluation of any tools used in safety-critical work. The activity can be analyzed from three distinct perspectives: performance, way of acting (habits of action, of knowing, and of collaborating), and user experience (UX) (discussed in more detail in Section 2.2.3). The **performance** aspect of analysis is focused on understanding the sequence of actions taken to carry out the tasks and arrive at the **outcome** achieved in the activity. However, the directly measurable human performance alone is not sufficient to indicate the appropriateness of the tools. Also, the **way of acting**—i.e., how the performance outcome is achieved—should be considered. This is because well-trained operators often can reach a good outcome even with poor tools and because of the fact that the operators themselves recognize that there are differences in ways of accomplishing the work and these differences might be meaningful in response to the general demands of the activity. The reference for the way of acting is the operators' orientation to the core task, because it assumes that the operators are attuned to the general safety-relevant characteristics of the domain while also executing the immediate process-control tasks. That orientation is demonstrated by the crews' ability to maintain a way of acting that enables reaching the objectives for the whole system. The third perspective of importance in analysis of the activity is acknowledgement of the user experience. Only a professional, an expert in the domain, can grasp the subtle implications that the tools may have in the activity. That is why the expertise of the professional operators can be usefully exploited in evaluation of the tools' appropriateness. This sense of expertise, involving professional user experience, as an indicator of the tool's development potential for use is just as valuable a perspective as the other two, mentioned above.

The stated understanding of the roles of the tools in activity and the three perspectives on observing and analyzing the usage activity can be applied to construct a definition of systemic usability (see Section 2.2.3). The notion of systems usability emphasizes the holistic nature of the attribute called "usability" while drawing on the object-oriented and mediating role of tools in an activity system. However, benefiting from the notion of SU in evaluation of HSIs calls for concrete indicators that express SU in practice. A two-dimensional matrix deriving nine general SU indicators on the basis of the three tool functions and the three perspectives on activity was presented in Chapter 2. These general indicators can be used in ascertaining more fully the relevant SU measurements for the context in question (see Figure 4.1). The successfulness of the activity in fulfilling the core-task functions is the evidence of a tool of good quality (i.e., systems usability), along with support for the individual tool functions.

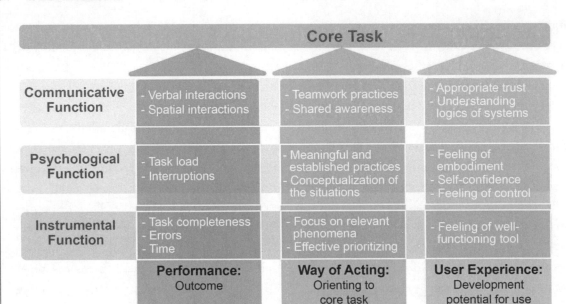

Figure 4.1: Nine specified classes of systems-usability indicators for NPP process-control work (Adapted from Savioja, 2014, p. 89).

4.2.2 MATURATION OF THE SYSTEMS-USABILITY CONCEPT IN THE DEVELOPMENT OF TOOLS

As the systems-usability approach indicates the level of appropriateness of a tool for an intended use and enables a systemic view of the usage of tools, it is interesting also from the tool-design and development perspective. The development of new control-room HSIs in the nuclear power industry is generally based on very conservative strategy. This leads to realization of HSIs that follow the same design philosophies and are based on the same design principles and guidelines as the existing ones, and the advances in modern HSI technologies are not able to be exploited fully. The more novel solutions often end up subordinated to the old, proven ones, so a situation arises wherein only minor improvements to the old system are implemented and enter use. Yet the notion of systems usability and especially the perspective of tool usage have pointed to positive user experience as an early indication of the success that could be achieved. The promise experienced in a new design solution can enrich the traditional design process for safety-critical systems. The user's feeling, even if not a well-formulated opinion so much as "gut feel" or a best guess of the usefulness of the technology at work, is meaningful from the design standpoint. It may be claimed that a positive emotion is evoked if the new technology is seen as bringing possibilities to develop the work and if it supports those elements of the work that the user considers worthwhile. In fact, one of the most important ways of anticipating the future use and the appropriateness of the tools to serve future work is the user's subjective evaluation of the potential of the tool. This is also a major motivation for aiming to measure UX. The ability to prove and document the emergent characteristics of the designed tool early on can be expected to ease the introduction of new technological support in the nuclear field.

The way from the drawing table to a finished product implemented in the control room is a long and time-consuming path. The process includes several iterations, checks and decision gates, and evaluation and validation activities, along with work contributions from many, quite different specialists. However, for the sake of brevity, four distinct phases can be identified in the design process (depicted in Figure 4.2). Design of a new tool/HSI starts with a phase that could be referred to as **idea generation**. In this phase, there is a strong orientation toward identifying possible future needs. Evaluation is required for creation of possible scenarios for the future work, but the reference for these evaluations is the core tasks. In the next phase, **concept design**, various technological options are considered and their promise for future concepts of operation is analyzed. Conceptual models are created for these purposes. It is vital that the evaluation not be too conservative, so that good design ideas are not turned down. At this stage, evaluation serves a truly innovative function and feedback for design is sought. In addition to the understanding of the content of the future work itself (i.e., the core task), the indicators of systems usability, especially UX indicators, become relevant. After concept design, more detail-level development of a design solution takes place. In this phase, which can be labeled **interface design**, the proposed concept is developed into tangible and more concrete form and the design solution or parts of it can be tested/experienced in use. In the interface-design phase, the evaluation typically focuses on prototypes and on specific parts or components of the final solution. Innovative evaluation is still needed in this phase, but normative or acceptance functions too enter the picture here, because fine-tuning and decisions are required with respect to the remaining open options. The intention is to gain confirmation that the design is proceeding toward a realisable end and that the requirements set are going to be fulfilled. It is in this phase that one can first develop an understanding of how the emerging tool functions in real use (e.g., with reference to the systems-usability approach's way of acting indicators). Finally, in the last main phase of the design process, the **integrated solution design** phase, the product is developed until it is in such a state that it can be tested (i.e., validated as a functioning system embedded in its context of use), in connection with a new concept of operations. In this phase, the evaluation focuses on the usage of the technology and the acceptability of the new tool from the end users' point of view. The SU indicators can be used in full scale for assessment of the quality of the final design (i.e., the capability of the technology to fulfill the functions of the tool in the activity) and to support fulfillment of the core-task functions in the intended work.

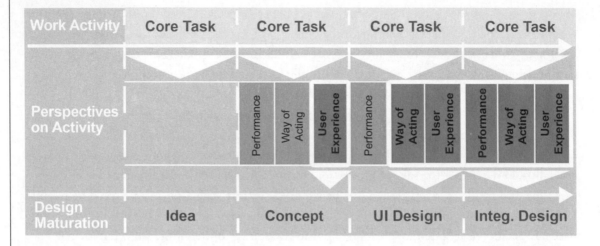

Figure 4.2: The design maturity of the tool in relation to the SU indicators and the development of the core task.

As is indicated above, the design process includes several phases that need to be taken into account when one is considering the progress of the product from the systems-usability perspective. Accordingly, evaluating the design solution and steering it in light of the systems-usability metrics established demands ability to cater to the longitudinal nature of the design and development of the tools. That means that several successive evaluations are carried out (in line with the design iterations) and that the results of an earlier evaluation round serve as a reference for the next evaluation (and, naturally, also offer seeds for further development of the design solution). The main reference, however, should be the claims as to the systems usability of the final product of the design and its support for the core tasks.

When one considers the object of the case study described here, the FITNESS control station, it is obvious that its design has not reached the final stage: that of an integrated design solution. Even though FITNESS is a comprehensive operator tool that is designed for interaction with an automated process, it is still operable and installed only in the development simulator environment. Moreover, while the system has a full HSI connected to a process simulator, this covers only the turbine-side operations and does not provide the necessary connection to the reactor-side processes. Accordingly, the FITNESS control station can be considered to represent a product that is in the concept phase and therefore far from being implemented in a real process-control environment. This phase is aimed at identifying and analyzing the potential of the proposed design solutions for future use. In the case of FITNESS, the interest is in understanding the promise that this novel HSI concept may hold and in gaining feedback indicating which of the innovative features built into it may be worth carrying forward.

It is the systems-usability frame in relation to which the innovative features of the design should be considered. Therefore, the focus in the case study is on the promise of FITNESS for future operator work, particularly with respect to user experience.

4.2.3   TOOLS-IN-USE MODELING OF THE FITNESS CONCEPT

The main designer in the development team for FITNESS, Dominique Pirus, summarized the design philosophy of the FITNESS simulator/HSI in the following terms: The FITNESS approach draws upon a generalization of the functional representation of the plant, which specifies the purpose of use of the plant functions in each individual situation. This approach enables the complexity of the process to be controlled in various respects. For example, the propagation of function failures from low levels to high functionality levels becomes clearer, which allows generation of a synthesis of reliable information on the availability of the key functions. In addition, the scheme of operations for commissioning (and decommissioning) the main functions during plant-unit start-up (and shutdown) becomes explicit and the operators are offered the possibility of carrying out related tasks in a more effective yet still flexible manner.

Even though the design process and the reasoning behind the various design solutions were described well by the designer, for the purpose of the concept evaluation it was necessary to conceptualize the specific innovative features that FITNESS may offer and that the operators were expected to experience and give their accounts of. Therefore, a **tools-in-use model** (see Table 4.2) was created for the FITNESS system by means of interviews with the designer and familiarization with (and analysis of) the available design documentation. The TiU model constructed aids in exploring the potential of the proposed system for process control work.

In the model, the core-task functions are situated in relation to the proposed design (innovative features) in a manner that allows examination and discussion of the value and the support the design may produce if implemented. When developing the model, we analyzed the work activity and the technological enablers, and we outlined the values incorporated into the future system, its major innovative features, and the operation of the system in practice. In other words, the resulting model presents the higher-level functional goals (e.g., the functional tasks of the human operators) in connection with the lower-level physical means (e.g., individual interface elements/partial design solutions) and allows viewing how the operators' activities and goals are supported in the context of their work.

The FITNESS TiU model emerged through several iterations and was also discussed with the designer. The concept description was then used for further planning of the FITNESS evaluation, training of the operators, and discussion of the content of the FITNESS concept with the operators in the course of the evaluation (e.g., in the focus-group discussion).

Table 4.2: The tools-in-use model for the FITNESS concept

FITNESS in process-control work					
Level 1: **Value/core-task functions**	Readiness to act • Operators are responsible for decision-making and supervision • Operators must be able to detect that an event has occurred	Narrowing of options and testing • Operators must be able to take over and adjust the system at any time	Interpreting and reorienting • Operators must be capable of identifying the causes and meaning of events	Concept-mastery and comprehending of wholes • Operators must understand the functioning of the automatic controls • Operators must have a global picture of the process	Creation of shared awareness • Operators apply the instructions in an intelligent way	Optimal sharing of efforts • Operators need flexible organization and division of tasks
Level 2: **HSI concept requirements**	Representation of the plant that is consistent with operators' view of the plant	Clearly evident relationships of process events to production or safety objectives		Automation level is adapted to operators' needs		
HSI concept solutions	1. Functional structuration of all kinds of displays	2. Functional structuration of synthetic information and alarms (available/unavailable, in service/out of service, and level of degradation)	3. Functional structuration and flexible automation of procedures			
Level 3: **Interface requirements**	Consistency of principles of operation in normal, disturbance, and emergency situations	Consistency of dialogs	Consistency of information presentation	Access to synthetic information at all levels	Transparency of the logic of how the system synthesises information	Freedom in accomplishing tasks and adjusting the level of automation

Interface solutions	Consistency of all operation and interface management dialogs • The same dialog principles are used for all plant situations, operation dialogs, and information\ Screen structuration is applied • Specific dialogs have dedicated areas	Inter-display links • There is a single operation/ monitoring/ procedure display for each function or component • The same vertical and horizontal structuration is applied across all types of displays	Information accumulation • Top-down access and navigation is used • Bottom-up access and navigation is used	Presentation of status information • Status information is integrated into the displays • Animated icons are used	Procedure system in flowchart format • Functional objective presented for each procedure • Use of animated icons	Functional structuration of alarm processing and presentation • Functional dynamic processing is used for the consequences of alarms for each function • Alarms are integrated into the displays • A functional synthetic view of alarms is presented for each function

Level 1 of the FITNESS model (see Table 4.2) presents the central content of the work (i.e., the core-task functions). The six core-task functions that had been considered in the earlier field studies to characterize the NPP operators' work (Norros and Nuutinen, 2005) were utilized as bases in the construction of the model specified for FITNESS. Beneath these general core-task functions, the demands of the operator work drawn from the FITNESS design documentation are depicted and listed in greater detail. These descriptions of the demands of the operator work mediate and could be seen as the designers' definition of the user requirements.

The FITNESS control station is depicted in the TiU model with regard to its innovative features in terms of the HSI concept and the user interface. In the middle and the lower part of the table, the HSI concept requirements and HSI concept solutions (see Table 4.2, level 2) and the interface requirements and interface solutions (see Table 4.2, level 3) are described in detail.

Four main HSI concept requirements and three HSI concept solutions for meeting those requirements were identified on the basis of the FITNESS documentation. The HSI concept solutions that were considered the central features for FITNESS were: (1) functional structuration of all kinds of displays; (2) functional structuration of synthetic information and alarms (available/ unavailable, in service/out of service, and level of degradation); and (3) functional structuration and flexible automation of procedures, i.e., the FITNESS mode of automation. The concept solutions are depicted in Figure 4.3.

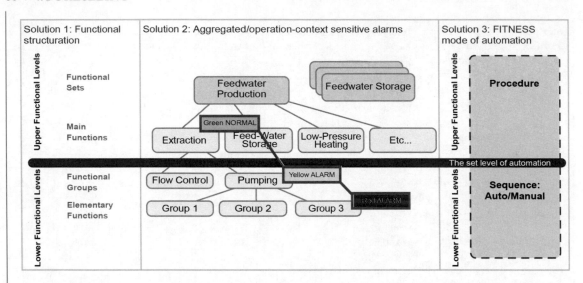

Figure 4.3: The three main concept solutions of the FITNESS HSI.

The first concept solution is the manifestation of the functional approach aimed at clarifying the operation objectives, along with the relations and interactions among the various plant functions, and making them explicit. In order to benefit fully from this function-oriented approach, the development team had to design a function structuration and place all displays, information, and alarms in a hierarchy (see Figure 4.3). For example, from the unique global plant-overview display, the operator can move down to the function level, at which the function-units/groups (e.g., seawater pumps) can be managed, and continue drilling down from there all the way to the lowest component level, where the elementary operation functions are performed (e.g., by individual pumps).

The second HSI concept solution listed above is functional structuration of synthetic information and alarms (see Figure 4.3). It represents a totally new kind of alarm philosophy, one that continues the function-focused approach introduced in connection with HSI concept solution 1. The novel alarm philosophy includes direct presentation of the alarms on the operator displays with a synthesized alarm indication corresponding to the function level considered. For example, an alarm will not be relayed with the same "severity index" throughout the display hierarchy; instead, the severity assigned depends on the function level at which the alarm is viewed. That is, the severity index takes into account all available redundancies, together with the contextual data related to the plant situation, hence assessing the need for the function subject to alarm. This way of presenting alarms should support the operators in identifying the causes and the meaning of the process events/disturbances (i.e., situation awareness) and facilitate interpreting in acting, which is considered the most appropriate way of acting (see Section 2.2.3).

Involving the concept of a FITNESS mode of automation, HSI concept solution 3 was based on the designer's understanding of what the optimal automation level would be in process-control work and how the joint human–automation operation should be organized (see Figure 4.3). The basic assumption is that the operators have the main responsibility for supervizing the process and they must be able to take over and adjust the system at any time. Automation's role is to make the operation more effective and adapt to the needs of the operators. Cooperation with the automation takes place through the computerized procedure usage.

These were also the main concept solutions whose promise for future work caught our interest and were subject to evaluation. The lowest level (level 3) of the FITNESS concept, as shown in Table 4.2, refers to the interface features that are more detail level means of promoting the overall aims of the FITNESS system through associated utility of the process-control operations. The description of level 3 is not exhaustive but suffices for the purposes of the evaluation described here and for understanding of the functioning of the FITNESS HSI.

4.2.4 FORESEEING THE POTENTIAL OF FITNESS THROUGH THE USABILITY-CASE METHOD

The content of the FITNESS TiU model—in particular, the three HSI concept solutions identified above (functional structuration of all kinds of displays, functional structuration of synthetic information and alarms, and functional structuration and flexible automation of procedures)—provided a focus for the evaluation. Here we utilized the systems-usability case approach that is under development for steering the fulfillment of SU targets in complex design and evaluation processes (see Section 2.2.3).

Formulation of Claims

First, claims pertaining to the FITNESS system were formulated in keeping with the logic of the usability-case method and case-based reasoning. The focus in development of the claims was on testing the relevance of the HSI concept solutions of the FITNESS system. Since this system is a control-station concept that is made material in the form of an interface (i.e., a prototype of the concept), the operators involved in testing the FITNESS system were able to experience the proposed concept solutions only through the simulator's interface. The most interesting claims to be tested in relation to evaluation of the promise of FITNESS (in the concept phase) were of three types:

- particular HSI concept solution supports fulfilling certain core-task functions;

- particular interface solution is the materialisation of the HSI concept solutions; and

- particular interface solution supports meeting of certain core-task functions.

The first and the third type of claims noted above are related to the operators' point of view (i.e., user experience), as there the interest is in the tool's capability of bringing added value to the work. The second type of claim is more design-internal. In it, the interest is more specifically focused on the adequacy of the lower level (user interface) solution for realization of the upper-level (HSI concept) solution.

For the sake of clarity, we demonstrate the evaluation of the FITNESS system's potential through examination of HSI concept solution 2, functional structuration of synthetic information and alarms. All told, eight claims were stated in connection with this solution, six of which were that a specific interface solution supports a particular core-task function (the third claim type) and two of which stated that a specific interface solution materializes a specific HSI concept solution (the second claim type). In Table 4.3, for clarity, only one of these eight claims is highlighted in a claim diagram.

Table 4.3: Formation of a claim that states a specific interface solution to support a particular core-task function (third claim type). This interface solution also materializes the proposed HSI concept solution (second claim type), and this HSI concept solution supports fulfilling the core-task claim (first claim type). (In the diagram, the dashed line represents the claim formation)

Level 1: Value Core Task	Readiness to act	Narrowing of options and testing	*Support for the core task* **Interpreting and reorienting**	Concept-mastery and comprehending of wholes	Creation of shared awareness	Optimal sharing of efforts
Level 2: HSI Concept Requirement	Representation of the plant that is consistent with operators' view of the plant	Components that are grouped into coherent sets and are interconnected	Relations of process events to production or safety objectives are made evident	Automation level adapted to operators' needs		
Solution	Functional structuration of all kinds of displays	*Is striven for through a concept solution* **Functional structuration of synthetic information and alarms (available/unavailable, in service/out of service and level of degration)**		Functional structuration and flexible automation of procedures		
Level 3: User Interface Requirement	Consistency of principles of operation in normal, disturbance, and emergency situations	Consistency of dialogs	Consistency of information presentation at all levels	Access to synthetic information	Transparency of the logic of how the system synthesises	Freedom in accomplishing tasks and adjusting the
Solution	Consistency of all operation and interface-management dialogs - The same dialog principles for all plant situation, operation dialogs, and information Screen Structuration - Dedicated areas for specific dialogs	Inter-display links - A single operator monitoring procedure display for each function component - The same vertical and horizontal structuration across all types of displays	**Claim** **Functional structuration of alarm processing and presentation (UI solution) supports/enables interpreting of acting and reorienting (core task) not allow exploiting the solution to its full extent** ...single type access and navigation	...ha ...iv ...h - Use of animated icons	*that is materialized by an interface solution.* **Functional structuration of alarm processing and presentation** - Functional dynamic processing of consequences of alarms for each function - Integration of alarms into displays - Functional synthetic view of alarms for each function	

Testing of Claims

Prior to the evaluation, the scenario runs, questions were phrased, and other supporting evaluation material were designed to address the specifics of the three main HSI concept solutions. Three distinct scenarios were selected for the evaluation. It was borne in mind that the scenarios should enable demonstration of the various innovative features of the FITNESS control station and should also include some disturbances, to challenge the operators and require some effort to identify the situation and find adequate operational solutions to manage and stabilize the process. The relatively small selection of scenarios available in the simulator constrained the final choice. When we considered the testing of the innovative features—i.e., the three main HSI concept solutions of FITNESS—it was necessary to ascertain which types of scenarios would be appropriate in the analysis of each of the features. Therefore, an attempt was made to make sure that each of these three HSI concept solutions could be tested in a scenario that would enable the feature in question to be called for during the scenario run. Also, the questions posed to the operators during the debriefing sessions were carefully designed to address those innovative features that were at the focus of each session. The debriefing questions (facilitated with pictorial material) addressed the specifics of the interface directly, as these were supposed to manifest the three HSI concept solutions and since the operators used the FITNESS interface to gain experience of the FITNESS concept. In Table 4.4, below, the evaluation material addressing HSI concept solution 2 is presented.

Table 4.4: Evaluation materials prepared to address the specifics of HSI concept solution 2

HSI Concept Solution 2. Functional Structuration of synthetic information and alarms

Scenario	Debriefing Questions	Pictorial Material	Focus Group
Scenario 4: Monitoring of the plant at 50% power with leakage in the HP heater. FITNESS mode Scenario 3: Conditioning of the steam lines with leakage in the HP heater. FITNESS mode	New way of alarm processing and presentation (a) 1) Did you make use of the new alarm processing feature during the scenario? 2) Did you have any problems in using the alarm processing and presentation feature? 3a) Did the alarm level build-uip features help you to understand the state of the plant and resources? 3aa) Did you find it easy to identify the functional level where an alarm appeared and the severity of the alarm? Presentation of the availiability and service status of functions (b) 3b) Did you find the availability and service status information helpful in judging the state of the process? 4) Did you have any problems in using the availability and services status information feature? 5) Is the alarm processing feature and the presentation of the status of functions very different from what you have been used to, and how? 6) Could this kind of synthetic information presentation bring added value to the operator work in the furture?		Discussion themes were built around the FITNESS TiU model and were focused especially on the value level (level 1) and the core-task functions connected to the HSI concept solution 2: -creating shared awareness - conceptual mastery and comprehending wholes - interpretativeness of acting - readiness to act In addition, the HSI concept requrements were discussed from the viewpoint of if the requirements corresponded the content of the work, i.e., core-task functions

Engaging operators in the scenario runs was followed by collaborative evaluation activities (e.g., debriefing and focus-group work), after which analysis of the collected data took place. The next step in the systems-usability-case reasoning was to find evidence from the data as to whether the claims about FITNESS would gain support. Of course, it was most likely that negative evidence would be gained for some claims and that many claims would remain without any evidence one way or the other. Notes of the researchers and the content of audio/video recordings (capturing operators' verbal reactions during the simulator runs and in the various interview and debriefing sessions) were transcribed for analysis and use as evidence in the testing of the FITNESS claims. Performance data (e.g., execution times) were not used as evidence in the evaluation of the promise of the FITNESS systems, since the focus was on operators' first impressions and the subjectively experienced value of the proposed system for process-control work.

To enable management of the linking of the evidence collected to the claims, the claims were expressed in verbal form and organized in a table, in which they were numerically ordered. After this, the evidence was connected to the claims via insertion of the individual pieces of evidence in the cells below the corresponding claims. On the basis of the evidence accumulated on each of the claims, arguments as to their fulfillment could be established. In Table 4.5, a sample of evidence pertaining to HSI concept solution 2 is provided. The example concerns the same claim referred to already in Table 4.3. In the claim diagram the gained support (positive evidence) for the claim is indicated by the weight of the connecting line.

Table 4.5: Evidence for argumentation on the example claim. Evidence is connected to the HSI concept solution and to the interface solution. The argument explains this evidence by saying that the HSI concept is found promising but that there are doubts about the way the interface is designed (in the diagram, the weight of the line represents the support gained for the claim).

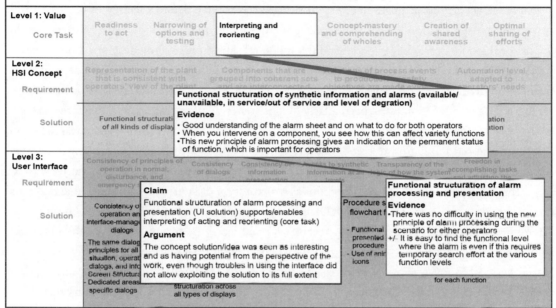

4.3   FINDINGS IN THE STUDY: EVALUATION OF THE FITNESS CONCEPT'S POTENTIAL

The results produced via the systems-usability-case documentation addressing the promise of the FITNESS system in operator work are presented next.

The concept solution 1 titled "Functional structuration and flexible automation of procedures" was the innovative feature that was most positively experienced by the operators and that also gained the most supportive evidence. This concept solution was considered to be well manifested by the interface solution "Procedure system in flowchart form." The automation solution of the FITNESS system was also found to support the requirement phrased as "Automation level is adapted to operator needs." Moreover, evidence was gained that features designed into the so-called FITNESS operating mode (i.e., operating in free order manually at upper function levels and in a specified sequence of operations automatically or manually at lower levels of system functioning) support the core-task functions of "Narrowing of options and testing" and "Optimal sharing of efforts." For example, operators experienced the FITNESS operating mode as reducing their workload since they could trust some of the operations to automatic systems. It also enabled an efficient way of working and thereby the experience of a well-functioning tool. Some doubt or caution was, however, expressed that automation according to FITNESS principles would be negatively manifested with regard to the core-task functions "Readiness to act" and "Concept-mastery and comprehension of wholes." In particular, the operators felt that operating in automatic sequence might lead to passivity that could act against acquisition of expertise and at worst give rise to a feeling of loss of control.

The concept solution 3, i.e., "Functional structuration of all kinds of displays," also gained the support of the operators. They experienced the functional structure as providing good presentation of the facility and as aiding in understanding the logic of the system and the interdependencies within the individual function levels. This concept solution was considered to be concretized in several innovative interface solutions, particularly " Consistency of all operation and interface-management dialogs," "Inter-display links," and "Procedure systems in flowchart form." There was, however, criticism expressed in relation to some usability aspects of these interface solutions (e.g., operators facing problems in recognizing the hierarchical levels of the display system while operating with it).

The concept solution 2 titled "Functional structuration of synthetic information and alarms" (used as an example above in Section 4.2.4, on foreseeing the potential of FITNESS through the systems-usability-case method) did not receive as much confirmatory evidence as the other two main concept solutions. That might be because the synthetic information and alarms feature was clearly the most innovative of the features, one with which the operators did not have any previous experience. Operators, for example, experienced difficulties during the scenario runs in reading the symbols indicating various kinds of status information and connecting these to the "severity index" determined by the current view of the display hierarchy. It was, however, promising that the evidence obtained was consistent with the use proposed or sought for the feature—i.e., that the functional structuration of synthetic information and alarms was found to be relevant to the core-task functions "Interpreting and reorienting" and "Concept-mastery and comprehension of wholes." The concept solution was also felt to be positively linked with the requirement that relations of process events to reaching of safety objectives be made evident. Therefore, it seems that the idea of providing a new kind of synthetic status of the plant as captured in this concept solution was seen as interesting and as having potential from the perspective of the work, even though the operators were not able to exploit the solution (as manifested in the interface) to its full extent.

The results show that it was natural for the operators to express opinions about the added value the solutions bring to their work. "Narrowing of options and testing" and "Concept-mastery and comprehension of wholes" were the two core-task functions that operators most often referred to as being positively affected by the FITNESS interface solutions. Other core-task functions too were seen as supported by the system, without more precise citing of the particular innovative feature of the system involved. On the basis of this small-scale evaluation, evidence was gained to support the conclusion that the FITNESS system is a promising innovation and was received well by the operators. The three main HSI concept solutions gained support, and their connection to the work demands (i.e., the promise of the solutions for future work) became evident in testing of the system.

4.4   CONCLUSIONS IN THE FORESEE-THE-PROMISE CORE-TASK DESIGN FUNCTION

How to foresee the promise of solutions (e.g., new tools and work methods) that do not yet exist and how they can be part of day-to-day work practices is a key issue. This chapter has dealt with recognizing the divergent yet possible development paths of future work in terms of potential activity and following through on the most promising ones for realization.

We have demonstrated the use of three methods to uncover the promise of solutions for future work: (1) the concept of systems usability as a comprehensive attribute to be aimed for in design and a quality to examine when assessing usability of a product or tool; (2) TiU modeling to discover and explicate the innovative features of the tool in relation to the work activity under development; and (3) the systems-usability-case method for its contribution to conducting a longitudinal review of the usability of a maturing design solution. Each of these methods in a unique way addresses the different characteristics of the evolving design or tool and is employed to uncover its potential to support future work.

The notion of systems usability offers a quality to be sought comprehensively in the design and development of new work systems. *Systems usability denotes the capability of the technology to fulfill the instrumental, psychological, and communicative functions of the tool in the activity, and to support the fulfillment of core-task functions in the work. Systems usability is evidenced in technology usage in an appropriate performance outcome, habits of action, and user experience.* Thus the notion of systems usability emphasizes the holistic nature of the attribute given the label "usability" and the systemic and mediating role of tools in an activity system. The SU indicators against which the new designs are evaluated express the promise contained in the proposed solutions.

Tools-in-use modeling as it embodies the concept of core task within an internal design logic (orientation of development toward problem-solution spaces) of a new product or tool aids in making the possibilities of the future work tangible. The model can be viewed both from the design perspective (e.g., what is the design rationale behind the proposed new product or tool?) and from the usage standpoint (e.g., how is the proposed new product or tool integrated into and supportive of the work practices of future users?).

The **systems-usability-case** method enables a process within which claims are defined with the aim of testing how well the product or tool fulfills the human-factors quality demands. It is worth reiterating that the quality sought in the usability case is labeled **systems usability**, indicating the technology's appropriateness for its targeted usage. The usability case is a reasoning process that takes the explicit form of an artifact (i.e., documentation) and serves as a mediator between the design process and the evaluation process. The usability case guides and captures the development of a product or tool from promising "concept" to professional and valued "tool."

The foresee-the-promise function draws together what is known about the work activity, the technological enablers, and previous usage experiences to make the organization of the future work intelligible and thereby open for stakeholders' value estimations (e.g., judgements as to whether the innovative concept is a promising tool for future work). It is also aimed at making the development process more transparent and rendering the reasoning behind the solutions created traceable. The methods demonstrated in this chapter through the example case provide means of dealing with the complexity involved in the design of a new product or tool for safety-critical work.

CHAPTER 5

Intervening: How to Develop the Work System

Work systems change all the time through people's activity. The complex and safety-critical work systems on which the Core-Task Design approach is especially focused are no exception to such change. Spontaneous changes are typically local and remain informal. The wider impacts of such changes on the work system are seldom observed or known, which is why they are preferably kept to a minimum by organizational routines. Respectively, when changes are being designed and implemented, comprehensive safety reviews and organizational routines are developed for the control of these processes.

The CTD approach is intended to support a well-mastered design process, but its particular mission is to enable the professional users' point of view to be incorporated into the design decisions and facilitate these users' creative contribution to the design. In the intervene-to-develop function, which focuses on the making of actual changes to the work system, the professional users have a strong role: without the input of these actors, there would be no renewed work process and new activity.

In this chapter, we reflect on how the intervene-to-develop function supported the human-factors impact on the NPP-related design work. On the basis of the experience gained so far, we will identify several types of interventions, discuss them, and elaborate on the methodological challenges they brought to the fore.

5.1 THE PRACTICAL PROBLEM IN THE EXAMPLE CASE

In the present chapter, we continue discussing the NPP automation and control-room renewal case. We will look at three separate studies in which we had the opportunity to intervene in the on-going design process and give our input to it. The intervene-to-develop design function becomes topical when solutions are sufficiently mature to be implemented in a real-world work process or when a particular solution that conditions further steps of the design needs to be tested. The question is how to strengthen the potential of the professional users to support the design in a design process that is complex and strictly constrained.

It is very important for future operations that the intervention test the appropriateness of the solution under design for its intended use. Therefore, the intervention should not be a linear process in which the expectations of the designers are simply verified and the solution confirmed as-is.

Instead, new knowledge of the solution should be obtained. That is why the intervention methods should be **formative**. This is a methodical quality requirement that has not been used to characterize evaluations, or training methods etc., in the nuclear domain. Instead, in these connections, the focus is on the traditional formal quality criteria of the methods employed. The latter criteria are necessary but may not be sufficient in the design context. Our proposal is to consider the criteria of a formative (i.e., developmental) intervention as introduced in Chapter 2 as further methodical criteria that development projects realizing the intervene-to-develop function should fulfill. These criteria are **use of external tools for double stimulation** (in Vygotsky's terms), **creative agency of participants**, **generalized knowledge as outcome**, and **participant control of the knowledge creation**. In the next section, we demonstrate how Core-Task Design works in carrying out the intervene to develop function such that the criteria for a formative intervention can be met.

5.2   FORMATIVE FEATURES IN THREE TYPES OF INTERVENTION WITH CORE-TASK DESIGN

In the intervene-to-develop design function, the human-factors experts, the engineering design team, and personnel of the relevant facility all collaborate closely. In the NPP case used here as an example, the researchers worked with the designers and plant personnel in several projects. The projects involved three types of interventions that may be interpreted as sub-functions of the intervene-to-develop function. These are **evaluation of human–technology systems**, **development of human competencies**, and **management of the human-factors design**. The following discussion examines three examples of these functions.

5.2.1   EVALUATION OF THE HUMAN–TECHNOLOGY SYSTEM

As has been indicated earlier, the renewal process being designed was to involve the existing analog I&C systems and the traditional hard-wired control room being replaced with new and modern, mainly digital systems. The scope of the modernisation was very extensive, with almost all of the current HSIs planned to be replaced with new HSIs. Other important characteristics of the modernisation were that the control-room solutions and concept of operations were strongly influenced by safety requirements and safety-criticality. The requirements for the solutions were set for combinations of process systems, automation, HSIs, human operators, and procedures that together perform the safety functions of the plant.

In a design commission of this sort, comprehensive independent verification and validation (V&V) activities to review the quality of the control-room design solution are mandatory. A widely used guide to accomplishment of such reviews is the human-factors engineering program review guide prepared by the U.S. Nuclear Regulatory Commission (NUREG0711, 2004). In the evaluation activities, we exploited general human-factors engineering (HFE) evaluation methods, but some adaptations and new features were needed to fit the methods to the specific case. It was found necessary to divide the verification and validation process into several steps, through which the focus was systematically directed to the individual parts of the control room and to each level of detail of the system. Only after these stages should the final step, the assumed integrated validation, be completed, covering the entire control room and looking at the activity of the crew in a holistic manner. The V&V process was, accordingly, designed to consist of pilot tests, sub-system validations (SSVs), and an integrated system validation (ISV) (Laarni et al., 2013, 2014). The overall structure of the validation concept and details of its accomplishment are provided in the reference works cited above (see Figure 5.1 for an overview).

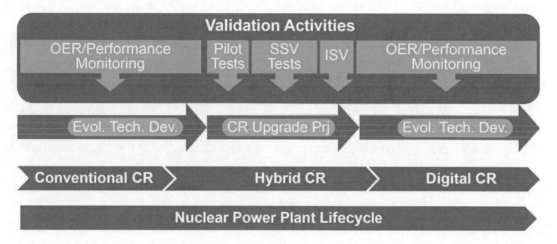

Figure 5.1: In the Loviisa NPP case the validation activities consist of SSVs = sub-system validations, and ISV = integrated system validation. These are part of the human-factors engineering process which is based on continuous monitoring of performance, i.e., OER = operating experience review. The human factors engineering process is embedded in the evolutionary technological development of the control room during its entire lifecycle (Laarni et al., 2014).

The sub-system validations can be considered most critical for providing feedback to design. Hence, the formative characteristics, including active participation of the process operators, should be particularly prominent in SSV methodology. The formative methodology also enables creating a concept of the developing whole while focusing on parts of the system. In the discussion that follows, we describe the means used to make the evaluation intervention a formative one.

Creative Agency of Participants

The validation tests for the control-room solutions required a large amount of preparatory work. When the interface designs were advanced enough to be tested, they were implemented in a design simulator that represents the NPP process on full scale. At the same time, emergency operating procedures to deal with possible accident situations were designed. The safety engineers designed test scenarios involving critical disturbance and accident situations. These scenarios were implemented for the simulator. The data collection and analysis methods and the execution of the test runs were carefully planned, and the operator crews from the power plant were invited to perform test runs with the simulated scenarios. The day before the tests, two trainers gave the operators full-day instruction in the interfaces to be tested, and detailed printed material on the interfaces was made available to them. The test runs were carried out on the next day. About 10 experts participated in each test session: observing the test runs were a simulator expert, two trainers, a designer as backup for informing about the designs, four human-factors experts and an expert in NPP operations, and finally 1–2 safety engineers.

All the effort described above for setting up the tests may raise the question of what is left for the operators to do. Is there room for open knowledge-creation during the tests? In reality, the situation with regard to the locus of control changes dramatically when the NPP's operation crew step into the simulator. The crew, consisting of the shift supervisor and two operators, take the main roles during the tests. The crew work independently in the control of several accident situations presented by the simulator. It is very impressive to see the crew take control of the process on the basis of their professional skills and knowledge. Through this process, the crew members observe how the new designs function as tools in their professional hands. Their judgement as to the appropriateness of the designs was the focus of the operators' participation, and they had also been instructed in this connection. The expertise-based participation of the crew in creating knowledge of the new tools under testing is very clear in its direction, and the results are beyond question; nothing can substitute for that input. But the creative agency was also strengthened by certain methodological means, which are described below.

Use of External Tools for Double Stimulation

One of the key features of the formative method is that actors in an intervention (in our case, the evaluation) not only face the actual problems of the task—i.e., the first stimulus (see Chapter 2)—but also are provided with conceptual tools to approach the problems. These tools constitute the second stimulus. What were the first and second stimuli in our case? The NPP operators are accustomed to working with the simulator, especially in training. On these occasions, they are instructed to handle the disturbances or other problems in the process that come as a surprise to them, i.e., their attention is directed to the first stimulus, the problems of the process. In consequence, the actors manage the disturbance and leave the session enriched by this experience of the process. An equivalent procedure is normally used in validation tests. In our validation sessions, we used a somewhat different procedure, with the aim being to focus the operators' attention on the tools used in operations. First, all the operators were informed about the type of process disturbance they were going to face, with the intention of avoiding too much focus being directed to the first stimulus. They were told that their role in the runs was to test the design and provide their expert opinion about the usefulness of the tools designed specifically for the process control. The operators were also informed that their observations would be discussed thoroughly after the session.

As a second measure for increasing the operators' agency in the evaluation we recorded the operators' actions carefully to enable their later joint reflection. Hence, during the activity (which lasted 20–40 min per scenario), each operator was shadowed by a human-factors expert who took notes on the operator's actions on paper reproductions of the displays or panels that the operator was using during the task. After the session, the researcher shared the notes with the operator and the two discussed all the operations and displays used during the activity. The discussion was at first a dialogue between the operator and his or her observer, while the other crew members actively listened. The latter were then asked to comment. This procedure was repeated with all three operator–observer pairs. The discussions were recorded and used as additional material in the analyzes that followed. Third, and finally, after running of the one-day test series, typically composed of three scenarios, the operators engaged in a group discussion, in which their focus was on the overall evaluation of the designs. The discussion was structured to focus on four main items: their evaluation of the successfulness of the process control, the novelty and safety-significance of the tools evaluated, the problematic and the positive features of these tools, and the effects of the designs on the concept of operations. It became evident in the discussions that operators did not always agree about the results of the tests with regard to the appropriateness of the specific features of the novel technology. But the operators were unanimous in their concern about the overall concept of operations that the new designs assumed. The increased role of procedures in coping with the demands of automation faced resistance especially, and the need for development of the team communication was expressed. These concept-level issues are difficult to address directly in tests; hence, this discussion provided a very significant contribution.

The instruction pertaining to the operators' focus in the testing, the augmented reflection on the use of tools, and the collective evaluation of the solution were the three tools that functioned as the second stimuli in the evaluation session. These enabled the operators and the researchers to create new knowledge of the designs tested, their usage, and the overall concept of operations.

Generalized Knowledge as Outcome

An important epistemic characteristic of a formative intervention is that the outcome of the intervention is not restricted to evaluation of the design in question, e.g., a particular sub-system; the lessons learned should be elevated to a higher level of abstraction. Such conceptually developed outcomes provide guidance to design of further parts of the system, or they may even be of help in creating solutions in new circumstances. In our case, ensuring the presence of this characteristic was very central, because the evaluations served the sub-system validations and the results were fed into a comprehensive cumulative knowledge base for acceptance of the whole control room for use.

In Chapters 2 and 4, we explained the concept of systems usability that we hold as the quality targeted, that representing a technology that is appropriate from the perspective of human factors. The design process should be steered towards systems usability, and the end product should fulfill the generic criteria therefor. It is assumed that good systems usability gives the personnel the capacity for reliable and safe acting. In this sense, systems usability is seen as supporting resilience of a system and, ultimately, supporting system safety.

A second version of the systems-usability case was developed to manage the complex evaluation process (the first version, explained in Chapter 4, is devoted to concept-design aims). The construction of a systems usability case for evaluation starts with defining the nine systems-usability requirements (see Chapters 2 and 4) in terms of claims that the system to be evaluated should fulfil. The human-factors design requirements determined in the design process for the system under evaluation are then analyzed and mapped to the nine systems-usability claims. These requirements are considered as sub-claims in the case. The results of the comprehensive simulator tests of the interfaces constitute evidence for testing the claims. In the systems-usability case the evidence are represented in the form of so-called human-engineering discrepancies (HEDs). The HEDs were strictly tied to the operators' actions and the researchers' notes on the tools discussed collectively during the tests. The HEDs indicate problems with the new design in use. Next, an argument is formulated that makes explicit the mechanism via which the evidence can be considered to challenge or invalidate the sub-claims and claims—that is, to endanger systems usability.

In consequence, three types of new knowledge of the interface are gained. First, when a relevant theoretical reference is sought for each of the design requirements, a review is conducted of how well the systems-usability qualifications are covered by the design requirements. Second, on the basis of the identification of HEDs, it is possible to identify how comprehensively the design requirements and systems-usability criteria are met by the actual solution. In our case, hundreds of HEDs were identified, showing that only a small number of design requirements did not receive negative confirmation. We could infer from this that certain aspects of systems usability were not achieved. Finally, when the HEDs are analyzed and arguments formulated to indicate mechanisms that hinder fulfilling of SU claims, new knowledge of the tool and its use is obtained. Classifications were created that organized the arguments emerging in the analysis.

The systems-usability case provided a conceptual "boundary object" that conveyed knowledge between the operators and the designers. It gave a systematic picture of the details of the solution in use and of how the outcomes of testing were related to the requirements set. The systems-usability-case work also accumulated information from one evaluation to the next as new evidence was received about the solution. The case can also be extended for consideration of new objects for evaluation. A systems-usability case aids in constructing and conveying understanding of the technology under evaluation and in building a shared view of its capabilities. Such an outcome is quite exceptional in validation exercises. These draw conclusions about of the solution's passing or failure of the test on the basis on the outcome of the crew's performance.

Participant Control of the Knowledge Creation

In a formative evaluation intervention, controlling the knowledge creation and exploiting the intervention's potential should not be the privilege of the researchers. On the contrary, the process operators, designers, trainers, and safety engineers should enter into productive dialogue during the intervention. They should appropriate models that could be used further as methods for continuing development. The experience of the series of evaluations conducted so far with the power company demonstrates the emergence of such a dialogue.

The input of the operators to the design has been judged by the designers to be a highly significant contribution. The transparency of the results achieved through building of the theory-based systems-usability case was considered a major improvement to the interpretation of performance-based human factors data. Each of the HEDs identified by the operators and articulated by the researchers was given a solution. The HEDs pertaining to the concept of operations were received in the design as an especially creative contribution, and design solutions and training solutions have been sought to improve the human–automation "teamwork," operator–operator collaboration, and the shift-supervisor leadership concept. A further significant creative contribution of the evaluation was operator training being placed on the design agenda. The evaluation sessions and the results produced therein were considered very informative also from the safety perspective. A decision was made to exploit the evidence created by the operators in the tests as a potential contribution to the general safety analyzes of the digitalized automation system.

5.2.2   DEVELOPMENT OF HUMAN COMPETENCIES

The second sub-function of the intervention-to-develop function was articulated as development of human competencies. As above with regard to the evaluation of the human-technology system, we will examine the matter from the perspective of a formative intervention. In this special case, the issue is related to development of a training program for the nuclear power plant operators of one Finnish NPP.

In Finland, nuclear power plant operators are required to hold a basic engineering degree. When entering employment with the power company, future operators receive three years of full-time operator training arranged by the company at the nuclear power plant. At the end of the training, a formal examination is needed for an operator's licence from the nuclear regulator. Specialists in various aspects of nuclear technology and nuclear safety carry out the classroom teaching in accordance with a set curriculum. The lecturers are not full-time instructors. Some of the training takes place in the full-scope training simulator on the NPP site. The simulator trainers are permanent full-time trainers who hold an operating licence and hence must have considerable experience of operator work. Additionally, one experienced operator at a time works as a simulator instructor for a fixed period to convey current experience from operations to training.

At the power plant considered here, the initial training for new operators was organized quite well, and the training program was based on international standards and guidelines. However, for example, the change of operator and instructor generation and also challenges caused by the modernization of I&C and control-room systems had prompted revamping of the initial-training system for operation personnel.

A developer from the training department of the plant was authorized to manage the training-development program, and she was our closest collaborator at the plant during several successive training projects. In the project described here, the present state of operation personnel's training at the NPP was analyzed. A detailed training curriculum was developed, but implementation was postponed. An overview of the project has been published with joint authorship by the plant representatives (Laarni et al., 2011). In this connection, we shall focus on reflecting on the formative elements of the training program's development.

Creative Agency of Participants

The professional users have a decisive role in a development study whose first key issue is to make a diagnosis of the situation and prepare a problem statement for the development project. The researchers visited the plant many times and gathered information on the training situation as comprehensively as possible. Interviews were carried out and workshops held with numerous people. Involved were operators who had recently finished the initial operator training; all of the simulator instructors; several managers involved with training, procedure development, and I&C renewal; the developers from the training department; and, finally, the plant's top management. Existing guidelines on operator training were reviewed, as were other relevant documents. Then, finally, the existing training material was reviewed and observation of training sessions carried out. The results of this analysis phase were written up in a comprehensive report, and a workshop was organized for discussion of the results and conclusions.

The diagnosis arrived at for the current training and its organization revealed the existence of contradicting goals that hindered the development of the training. The following key challenges and tensions with respect to operator training were articulated.

- There exists a tension between the regulatory requirements guiding trainees in rote learning and mechanical studying to pass the official exams, on one hand, and experiential reflective learning aimed at internal exploration and examination of key issues.

- The central problem in learning to operate the NPP is that the trainees have difficulty in structuring and remembering the extremely numerous details that they need to know.

- Because appropriation of the required knowledge and skill is very troublesome, the trainees experience difficulties in building sufficient self-assurance and courage to act even in the simulator conditions, let alone taking on the role of responsibility of the operator.

The generalized comprehension of the situation gained was used as the starting point for training-program development (via the "vision") for which tools were created (discussed in the following sections).

Use of External Tools for Double Stimulation

The training-related problems described above represent the first stimuli in the intervention for development of training. The further work was accomplished by a development group composed of eight simulator instructors and developers, working alongside three researchers. The development group then started to work on the renewal of the NPP-operator initial-training program. In proceeding to solve the problems identified in line with the logic of a formative intervention, we provided conceptual tools for approaching the problems. These tools constituted the second stimuli. The following types of tools were in use.

Modeling of operator work
The comprehension of the core task of the operator work was the starting point for the reflection on the operator training. In the workshops held with the development group, the researchers described process operation work with the aid of international studies and their own empirical studies. These empirical results were summarized with the aid of the core-task functions model (see Chapters 2 and 3). The development group were also confronted with the differences in their ways of understanding the core task, by means of the results of the work-orientation interviews conducted earlier with the participants themselves. Additionally, the development group compared their own understanding of the operator work to results that had been gained earlier with a much larger sample of NPP operators in Finland (Norros et al., 2014).

Definition of training targets
A further second stimulus used was a structured method borrowed from the literature for development of training content. The session in which training targets were conceptualized began with a review of the results from the analysis of the tensions manifested in the current operator training: The following issues were agreed on for the integrative ideas to be implemented in the training targets and content definition:

- interaction between theory and practice in training;

- comprehension of the process as a whole during training;

- combining individual-level and collective learning;

- observing the constraints related to the timing and order of training units; and

- monitoring and support of learning.

Two groups, of four people each, were formed. These began designing the basic structure of the training program on the basis of the above-mentioned tools and specifications, coupled with the instructors' expertise with relevant training contents. The two groups were also equipped with descriptions of the current NPP operator initial-training program.

Generalized Knowledge as Outcome

A formative intervention is assumed to produce outcomes that are not applicable only to the particular innovation task at hand. The outcome is a kind of vision of the new work with regard to the issue studied. Hence, the outcomes typically also encompass conceptually fleshed out ideas that provide guidance in the design of further solutions, in new circumstances. Can we claim that such results were achieved in the training-development project? The answer is "yes": the concept for the NPP operators' training that the development group produced is a generic outcome of the training-development project. The concept for the initial training is depicted in Figure 5.2.

This concept entails a new generic structure for NPP-operator training. The structure now in place is designed to serve certain, partially outdated production aims (e.g., trainees are occupied with some production tasks during their three-year training period). The new concept observes the integration principles mentioned above; for example, it takes into account the need for interaction between theory and practice, and it supports comprehension of the process as a unified whole during training. Practical field training, simulator-based training, and new qualification requirements for the relevant members of the profession represent different aspects of practical training, and these were meshed with the more theory- or system-oriented content of the training in a balanced way. This new structuring was also aimed at supporting comprehension of the dynamics of the process holistically. The new training program would also broaden the future operators' view from a technology perspective to encompass the organizational and production perspectives also.

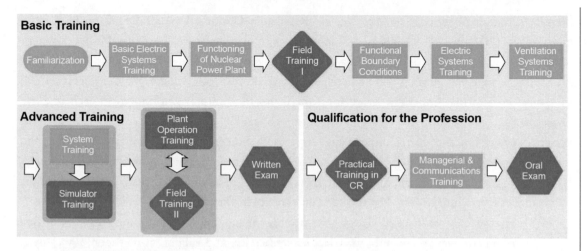

Figure 5.2: An outline of the initial operator-training system (Laarni et al., 2011).

The proposed new concept for NPP operators' initial training is a generic concept that requires a great deal of further work and enables diverse solutions.

Participant Control of the Knowledge Creation

The development team worked highly autonomously, and the participants were allowed to devote a considerable number of their regular working hours to this activity. The development project completed provided one detailed curriculum solution able to actualize the main concept. After the development team, in which the researchers too were involved, as facilitators, had delivered an example curriculum that followed the overall structure specified, the development work for renewal of the operator training was left to the company.

The work of the development team had even further impact within the organization. Equipped with the conceptual support of the development program in the advances made for the training program, a part of the team became responsible for the development of an extensive operator-training program responding to the digital I&C and the corresponding new concept of operations. A further development project is planned, for improvements to learning in daily operative work and practical simulator exercises. As a first step in this effort, a guidebook to support on-the-job mentoring practices has already been developed.

5.2.3   MANAGING THE HUMAN FACTORS IN DESIGN

From the very beginning of our collaboration with the NPP in relation to the modernisation of the plant I&C and control-room systems, it was clear that there is need for overall management of the human-factors activities during the design process. This management effort is often called human-factors engineering. The U.S. Nuclear Regulatory Commission's guidelines on HFE program review (NUREG0711, 2004) were identified as an important starting point for development of new methodology (Norros and Savioja, 2004). It was emphasized that HFE should take place in four separate phases: planning and analysis, design, verification and validation, and operation and in-service monitoring. Guidance is given on the issues that must be monitored in each of these phases, and 12 HFE issues in all were to be considered: HFE program management, operation-experience review, functional requirement analysis and function allocation, task analysis, staffing and qualifications, human-reliability analysis, human–system interface design, procedure development, training-program development, human-factors verification and validation, design implementation, and human factors' monitoring (see the 12 framed boxes in Figure 5.3).

The power company acknowledged the need for managing human-factors design, but first the primary motive was to create human-factors verification and validation methodology to meet the specific demands of the renewal process (see above Figure 5.1). Later, the company recognized that HFE should actually be taken as a broader issue and a perspective complementary to the engineering design. This conclusion was facilitated by the fact that a human-factors specialist joined the design group. She was made responsible for developing an HFE program for the company. This new focus was motivated also by forthcoming updates to the design requirements that the Finnish nuclear regulator was preparing.

Our human-factors research team supported the development of an HFE review approach (Salo and Savioja, 2014). This collaboration demonstrates another design intervention that should fulfill the criteria for a formative intervention, among other requirements. The related intervention actions are described next. Again, the four criteria for a formative intervention are used as a reference in the description.

Creative Agency of Participants

The engineering competence needed in the design and operations of nuclear power plants is known to be of a high standard. Against this reference, the mastery of human-factors engineering was known to be less developed, but the actual awareness of HFE on the part of the regulator or the utilities was not known. The intervention was, therefore, begun with an analysis of the situation in which personnel both from the Finnish nuclear regulator and from the nuclear utilities were involved. An interview-based study was conducted within the regulatory body on their guidance and oversight with respect to human factors in the design of nuclear facilities (Savioja et al., 2011). It turned out that, at the time of the interviews, no agreed conception of HFE existed and no processes or workflows of regulatory oversight focused on it. However, the need for HFE oversight had been identified within the regulatory organization. A clear indication of this was that HFE was planned for introduction to the revised nuclear guidelines that were under preparation at the time.[5]

Awareness of the necessity of HFE review was much greater at the power company with whom we worked. Because the company has an in-house design department that is involved with projects in other companies, they have felt a need for human-factors review guidelines that would comply with the international standards and guidelines and that would be relevant for the guidance of their design processes and practices. A small development team was established, composed of the human-factors specialist from the design department and one human-factors researcher. The team was authorized to outline an HFE design program for the company. It was clear at the outset that the work would be challenging. One of the goals was simply to make HFE a more prominent discipline within the company. Another was for the working group to convince the designers and the company's management of the added value of HF work in design.

As in our other interventions, there was a need for considerably in-depth diagnosis of the situation at the company. The development team carried out a series of interviews within the nuclear power plant and in the design department, with the intent of ascertaining the potential role of HFE in various project phases. The group also wanted to demonstrate the links between HFE and other design disciplines.

Use of External Tools for Double Stimulation

The double-stimulation element in this intervention project consisted of the NUREG-0711 conception of the 12 human-factors review issues (again, see the 12 framed boxes in Figure 5.3). The template provided in NUREG-0711 was designed for review rather than for design purposes, but it was still found to be the most adequate starting point for devising of the HFE design program. The development team analyzed the interview data collected and mapped the HFE-related activities found for the plant to the 12 HFE functions specified in the template. The resulting mapping is depicted in Figure 5.3.

The results showed that many of the activities proposed by the guidelines were already in place at the plant but not articulated as HFE activities and that integration among the activities was absent.

---

[5] The new guidelines have recently entered into force and include the recommendations of NUREG-0711.

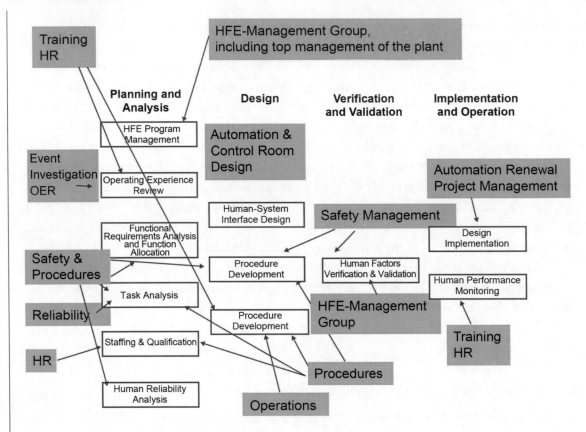

Figure 5.3: Mapping of the existing human-factors-engineering-related activities (in shaded boxes) of the nuclear power plant to the 12 HFE issues referred to in the NUREG-0711 review guidelines (in framed boxes) (figure obtained in personal communication with Savioja and Salo). HR = human resource, OER = operational experience review.

Generalized Knowledge as Outcome

Drawing from the results of exploiting the NUREG-0711 template for interpretation of the interview data, the development team started to sketch a human-factors engineering program for the power company.

A model of the HFE process is depicted in Figure 5.4. As the figure indicates, the HFE program has five separate phases, which comply with the general engineering design process model utilized at the company. These phases are preliminary clarifications, requirements' definition and conceptual design, basic and detailed design, verification and validation, and in-use monitoring. For each phase, specific inputs, HFE activities, and outputs are detailed in the program document. As Figure 5.4 indicates, the phases are meant to be iterative when this is necessary: in the case of emergence of new knowledge—on such matters as requirements or constraints—the previous phases are repeated to the necessary extent.

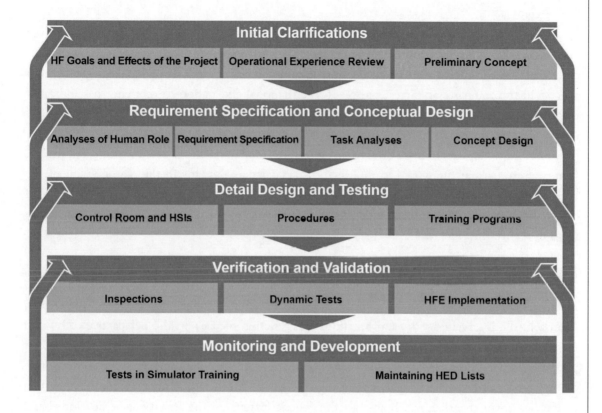

Figure 5.4: Schematic presentation of the power company's human-factors engineering program. The main phases and content are taken from the work of Salo and Savioja (2014).

The HFE program model described above was introduced in a more detailed written document. This describes the general goals of HFE, specifies which organizational resources are responsible for the HFE, and explains the management process for HFE. These explications are very important for the embedding of the HFE program in the company's other design and management activities.

The company's HFE program model is a design model that diverges from the NUREG-0711 review guidelines in three main respects: First, this model is embedded in the overall design process, which is not the case under NUREG-0711. Second, it features a concept-design phase during which the initial ideas surrounding design solutions are documented. Third, and finally, it describes a design process that is iterative in nature and in which each round of iteration adds to the level of detail of the design solutions. Also, rather than being developed for a specific project, the program is designed to be a general framework for various kinds of projects (Salo and Savioja, 2014).

Participant Control of the Knowledge Creation

The intervention consisting of the development of new HFE practice for the nuclear power company must be considered a phase preparatory to a potentially more comprehensive development process in the company's design department. International and national experience has indicated that the design of automation and instrumentation is a very complicated issue in a safety-critical industrial organization. It may be expected that there is a need for integrated design of NPP control, entailing an understanding of the technical and the human resources as a joint object of design. It appears to us that the work accomplished in our partner company in the development of the HFE program could be a significant contribution to a more fully integrated approach to design of automation systems. The company's designers and the management are the main agents in future work to realize this potential.

5.3 CONCLUSION

In this chapter, we demonstrated the third design function entailed by the Core-Task Design approach: the intervene-to-develop function. This function focuses on the perspective of how to transform a given actual activity into a new actual activity by further development of the foreseen potential activity. One may expect such a transformation to be troublesome and to present contradictory processes in which resistance to change too exists. This design function exploits the results of the two covered earlier, which abstract the generic features of the activity to be developed and represent an attempt to foresee the potential that exists for the development of the activity. In both of those design functions, the researchers also collaborate with the professional users. With the intervene-to-develop function, that collaboration must be developed even further, as the third design function involves making the actual changes in the work. It is important for the professional users to be seen as the key actors of the function, with their creative efforts supported by researchers or other specialists.

In the intervene-to-develop function, the interplay between the intentional and the structural orientation in research becomes part of an effective learning and development method that has been labeled the formative intervention. In summary, a formative intervention is an open learning and innovation process facilitated by certain structural elements deliberately designed into the process. Four elements or features were named that characterize a formative intervention: the participants' creative agency, use of external tools for double stimulation, generalized knowledge as outcome, and the participant control of the knowledge creation.

Three sub-functions—evaluation of the human-technology system, development of human competences, and management of the human-factors design—were identified within "intervene-to-develop," and examples of these were presented. The examples reveal quite extensive development processes that have been completed by the nuclear power plant with the aid of human-factors researchers. It appears to us that we have succeeded in organizing the human-factors support on the basis of the features of a formative intervention. In all sub-functions, the creative agency was realized via extensive involvement of the professional users in ethnographic studies to identify the present problems that the intervention was planned to deal with. The problems were tackled in development groups with the aid of models provided by the researchers that enabled the users to construct novel solutions. The outcomes of the interventions were not local solutions only; they always included a generic concept that could be used in development of new specific solutions. Finally, the professional end users and the company appropriated the concepts developed and grew to become independent agents of the change processes that had commenced but not nearly finished within the interventions.

Further, we see that the interventions accomplished have demonstrated that the great effort that ethnographic studies and the development of models for the work entailed was truly justified, in that they have made a clear contribution to the development of the work. The exercise also revealed that, from a developmental research perspective, we could considerably improve the intervention methods and the design of the intervention sessions. The interventions involved in future development processes could bring in even more determined facilitative activity on the researchers' part in preparation of the design sessions and in finding ways to increase the involvement of the professional users in filling the developer role and fulfilling the associated responsibilities. This developer role needs to be incorporated into the operational culture of the NPP, and the associated feature should be one element of the plant's safety culture. The management have a decisive role in promoting such an extension of the safety culture.

CHAPTER 6

Core-Task Design in Broader Perspective

In this book, we focused on developing the Core-Task Design approach with the aim of increasing the impact of human-factors expertise in the analysis, development, and design of work. It was mentioned in the introduction that the role of human factors in design is currently subject to lively discussion within both the human-factors/ergonomics and the human–computer-interaction community. In both traditions, there appears to be increased interest in developing more systemic or holistic approaches that could provide better support for the design of future work. In addition to responding to this interest, we have outlined some of the global changes in the socio-technical foundation of modern society that contribute to the current trend of both work and day-to-day life growing more systemic, dynamic, and networked. Our aim here has been to participate in this discussion by first focusing on the obstacles internal to the human-factors discipline that impede it from becoming more useful in future design.

In this final chapter, we are at an appropriate juncture to set Core-Task Design in a wider perspective. The message we aim to convey is that the proposed improvements in human-factors methodology are valid also more broadly in the design of future technology and services, and that the enhanced methodology could make a contribution to a new design culture.

6.1   THE MOTIVE FOR THE CORE-TASK DESIGN APPROACH

In a sense, the Core-Task Design approach is a by-product of the work that we, in our human-factors team and with many industrial collaborators, have accomplished with the intention of solving practical problems in modern, complex work. Yet this is not the whole truth. We have also had an articulated aim of accomplishing scientific work on theoretical and methodological problems of human activity in order to understand the phenomena that lie behind the practical problems of work and to create better methodology grounded tools designed to solve them.

The practical context of our scientific endeavour almost forced us to proceed from human factors that could be characterized as contextual. We needed an approach to human social and individual-level activity that acknowledges that the patterns and features of this activity cannot be understood in isolation from the context in which it takes place. Taking this as a starting point made it evident that human-factors research practice needs to be multidisciplinary; experts in the social sciences have to work alongside researchers from the fields of engineering, information technology, and arts and design, in order to be competent to interact with professionals in the various work domains of interest. Important means to facilitate the multidisciplinary interplay are the conceptual models created of the designed work.

The underlying fundamental orientation to a contextual approach helped us to take seriously the problems we encountered in applying a human-factors approach in analysis and design of work. If we want to be useful in design, we must find concepts and methods that capture the problems specific to each work setting, but at the same time we need to identify the generic mechanisms that lie behind the problems. Moreover, it is necessary that the concepts and methods tackle the problems at such a level of granularity as lends itself to solving the problems in design. Some of the generic problems we encountered were summarized in the introductory chapter. And, as we wrote, the diagnosis was that, if we are to improve the capability of human-factors practitioners in design, there is a need to develop the unit of analysis, so that both the social and the physical environment in interaction with human intentions are considered in the efforts to explain the phenomena of the work activity. The practice-theory approach provides a broad methodological framework for human-factors research appropriate to our aims. From among the multitude of practice-theory approaches we focused on those that are particularly suitable for our research aims and that clearly demonstrate a "family resemblance" from one to the next.

6.2   THE HUMAN-FACTORS CONTRIBUTION OF CORE-TASK DESIGN

In this section, we reflect on the Core-Task Design approach within the frame of human-factors research. We will highlight three merits of Core-Task Design that we consider to constitute significant improvements to the present approaches taken in human-factors research.

6.2.1   NEW VOCABULARY FOR EMPIRICAL ANALYSIS OF PRACTICE

For changing the perspective of human-factors research, a methodological decision was made to adopt the concept of practice as the unit of analysis. For this choice to be effective in empirical research, we also needed to propose some more specific concepts for further operationalization of the practice concept in pursuit of the aims of that research. Therefore, a new vocabulary was developed for use in the analysis of practice. The key innovation in this connection lies, first, in that the possibilities the environment provides for activity and the functions of technology as tools are described with the aid of various functional modeling methods. Thereby the core task is defined, with the assistance of which the actual activity is studied via detailed ethnography and in light of the orienting mechanisms of activity—i.e., work orientation and habit. These mechanisms express the logic and ways of exploiting the possibilities of the environment, and they reveal the connection of actions and operations to the motive for acting and uncover the meaning of behaviors in the specific work situation at hand. The analysis of actual activity develops the understanding of the core task further. We consider these features of the methodology to enable bridging between the societal and environmental structuring of activity and the intentional determination of activity.

6.2.2   THE HUMAN-FACTORS DESIGN MODEL DEVELOPED

The theoretical and conceptual work accomplished in developing the CTD approach was very necessary, but the outcomes of it would remain internal to the human-factors community if the picture were not completed with a further contribution. This contribution is more directly connected to the articulated needs of those who would apply human-factors expertise for design or practical development of work. It is the proposed Core-Task Design model, which describes the way of addressing the human factors in design. The three functions that we identified in the model, which we gave the names "understand-to-generalize," "foresee the promise," and "intervene- to-develop," enable human-factors research to comprehend activity from three distinct perspectives—in terms of the actual as abstracted to the core, potential, and new actual. As the case studies we used as examples have shown, one of these functions may be at the focus of the research while the other two are in the background; however, all three are present. It is for this reason that the model deals with three functions of design rather than describing three phases of a design process.

6.2.3   METHODS FOR DEVELOPMENTAL AND PARTICIPATORY DESIGN

The Core-Task Design model draws on epistemology that acknowledges the central role of practical acting on the object of work in construction of knowledge of the object. This epistemic premise is among the features common to the practice-theory approaches. Nevertheless, it has been claimed (Kuutti and Bannon, 2014) that, by and large, practice-theory approaches are strong in explaining activity but weaker for development of activity. The clear exception is, of course, the cultural-historical theory of activity, of which emphasis on development is a hallmark. The Core-Task Design model has gained much from CHAT-based developmental work research (Sannino et al., 2009), but we find CTD to complement the methodological apparatus of developmental research into work especially through the conceptual and methodological tools for analysis of the environmental structuring of activity and via exploitation of the intentional dynamics of actual activity in technologically highly mediated work.

The challenge for the human-factors discipline in design is to let the users take an active role in creation of the solutions while still providing guidance to the change processes, monitoring their course, and developing new solutions. Our conclusion in the CTD approach is that the researchers must master and apply ethnographic methods for allowing the professional actors' voice to be heard and their intentions to be taken seriously. At the same time, there should be some generic and predefined structure that provides a more general perspective to the analysis. We can see that both the use of ethnographic methods and structuration of the generic features of the activity are better in CTD than what is seen currently in mainstream human factors work.

6.3 STRIVING FOR A NEW DESIGN CULTURE

In the introductory chapter of this book, we mentioned three global changes in which the nature of future technology, work, everyday services, and living environments is thought to crystallize. These are the rapid changes seen in operating environments, improvements in efficiency and product/service quality, and increase in the complexity and networked nature of socio-technical systems. Since these changes extend globally in the diverse activities of the networked information society, it appears natural that human-factors research intended to support design also has a global character. For many years, it has been usual to distinguish between research that focuses on human activity in work and that focusing on people's use of computer-based everyday tools. In today's circumstances, it appears realistic to withdraw from this distinction and to strive to develop research approaches that capture the shared challenges faced by people everywhere and in every role in which they act with technology, whether as producer, consumer, or prosumer. The challenge is to develop design theories, models, and practices—in fact, a wholly new design culture—that captures in an efficient and appropriate manner the demands that arise from the global changes listed. Figure 6.1 presents a visualisation of the situation in which design activity currently finds itself. The figure demonstrates that a new manner of design, a new design culture, must be created that has at least two important capabilities: creating resilience and producing an integrated process.

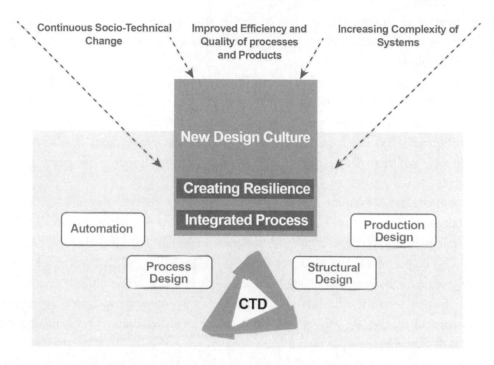

Figure 6.1: The new design culture develops in response to changes in future work. The new design approach integrates various design tracks, including Core-Task Design for human factors.

6.3.1 DESIGNING FOR RESILIENCE

The first key capability of the new design culture is the ability to create solutions that enable balancing between stability and flexibility (Grote, 2012). This would mean that, simultaneously with the technical and organizational solutions, by such means as automation and procedure control, enabling standardised and controllable services and environments, these solutions also provide possibilities for flexible and adaptable functioning of the technology and human actors. The capability for adaptation, which has been labeled resilience (Hollnagel et al., 2006), is needed as a complementary capacity in all environments that change continuously and may also bring unexpected events the design did not anticipate. These environments exist in all arenas of human life, ranging from work to leisure and the home. Creating resilience into the systems is a great challenge for design.

6.3.2 CREATING AN INTEGRATED DESIGN PROCESS

The second key capability that design should possess in the future is that of forming an integrated design process in which the diverse design streams, tasks, and disciplines may communicate, collaborate, and coordinate their activities in an optimal way (Papin, 2002). Among these design streams or activities are structural design, process design, automation design, and organizational and human-factors design. The object of integrated design activity is the entire socio-technical system, not just the technology.

Advances in exploitation of the Internet of Things, development of the remote operation and automation employed in production and service provision, the use made of robots and teamwork with robots, etc. require system-oriented approaches to design and, accordingly, also consideration of the role of human actors in the concepts of operation of these technologies. It follows from this that human-factor expertise must be incorporated into design much more profoundly and widely than it is today.

We could cite as an example the so-called Smart Cyber-Physical Systems (CPS) that the European Union has identified as one of the significant research topics in the current EU Research and Innovation program Horizon 2020. The program materials refer prominently to knowing, doing and being: cognition beyond problem solving' (H2020, 2014, p. 4) that is aimed at renewing ties between the many disciplines studying knowledge, cognition, and related issues (embodiment, development, insight, identity, responsibility, culture, etc.) from various perspectives (e.g., the neural, physical, social, and ecological), with special emphasis on artificial cognitive systems beyond the level of dull task-execution or repetitive problem-solving. This topic has been selected "to stimulate new interdisciplinary configurations and for its potential to boost future innovation potential in robotics, materials and cyber-physical systems" (H2020, 2014, p. 4).

One of the emerging trends in engineering design methodology that are expected to give answers to the challenges of future designing of complex Cyber-Physical Systems is the development of model-driven engineering. Well-defined models of both systems and engineering processes should take a decisive role in such engineering activity (Tommila et al., 2013). Core-Task Design, in its way of exploiting multiple models of socio-technical system functioning, should provide grounds for integrated model-driven systems engineering.

6.4 CONCLUSIONS: CORE-TASK DESIGN IN THE NEW DESIGN CULTURE

We claim that Core-Task Design is an approach within the human-factors discipline that has capacity for involvement in the development of a new design culture.

As a contextual approach, CTD maintains an interest in communicating both with engineering disciplines that focus on the technology and the physical environment and with the social sciences, which deal with the social environment. The CTD approach brings an ecological perspective to modeling instead of restricting the modeling of human conduct to reductionist models that follow technical analogies. Conceptualization of the core task is the central result of this elaborated functional modeling.

With the aid of the functional models of the joint human–technology–environment systems, CTD is capable of dealing with values that the activity of the system expresses or should strive for. Making the values explicit throughout the design process also enables traceability.

Well-developed ethnography plays a central role in Core-Task Design methodology. The methodology exploits both traditional methods and its own techniques for comprehending how people act in real-world situations. What CTD provides beyond the contribution of many other ethnographic approaches is found in its attempt to abstract the generic systemic connections and developmental principles that render acting in the environment appropriate and make the human–environment system viable. Revealing the orienting mechanisms in behavior and articulating the power of an interpretative relationship with the environment are the key achievements of CTD with which it can define targets for resilient acting and tools that support it. The consideration of the general aspects of the activity enables escaping from the task–artifact cycle and developing solutions that both mesh with the current ways of working and provide opportunities for development.

Finally, Core-Task Design supports the new design culture by drawing attention to the important role of the design thinking in creation of new knowledge. Rather than seeing design as mere application of knowledge, CTD considers design to create new knowledge about technology in practice. In consequence of this epistemic stance, CTD values the role of professional users in the innovation of new technologies, work, or living environments. Here, too, CTD goes beyond many of the existing approaches—in particular, human-centered design. The implementation of CTD does not restrict itself to individual- and situation-specific reactions of professional users; instead, it enhances the reflective development of practices in which the professional users are engaged in dialogue with developers. That dialogue is organized and facilitated through the offering of concepts with the aid of which the solutions are developed as generic conceptual solutions extending beyond the particular design task and situation or the opinion of a single user. Such participation of the professional users is meant to transform the reality and to develop capabilities to continue this change, as the future work and everyday living require.

Bibliography

Amalberti, R. (2006). Optimum system safety and optimum system resilience: Agonistic or antagonistic concepts? In E. Hollnagel, D. Woods, and N. Leveson (eds.), *Resilience Engineering: Concepts and Precepts*. pp. 253–71. Aldershot: Ashgate. 8

Automation (2010). *Valvomo - Suunnittelun Periaatteet ja Käytännöt [The Control Room—Principles and Practices of Design]*. Helsinki: Suomen Automaatioseura ry/Finnish Society for Automation. 6

Bennett, K.B. and Flach, J.M. (2011). *Display and Interface Design: Subtle Science, Exact Design*. Boca Raton, Florida: Taylor and Francis. 36

Bishop, P. and Bloomfield, R.A. (1998). "Methodology for Safety Case Development." Paper presented at the Safety-Critical Systems Symposium, Birmingham. DOI: 10.1007/978-1-4471-1534-2_14. 39

Bjørkli, C., Övergård, K., Röed, B., and Hoff, T. (2007). Control Situations in High-Speed Craft Operation. *Cognition, Technology and Work*, 9(2), pp. 67–80. DOI: 10.1007/s10111-006-0042-z. 30

Bourdieu, P. (1990). *The Logic of Practice*. Cambridge: Polity Press. 22

Boy, G.A. (2013). *Orchestrating Human-Centered Design*. London: Springer. DOI: 10.1007/978-1-4471-4339-0. 44

Carayon, P. (2006). Human Factors of Complex Sociotechnical Systems. *Applied Ergonomics*, 37, pp. 525–35. DOI: 10.1016/j.apergo.2006.04.011. 26

Carayon, P., Wetterneck, T.B., Rivera-Rodriguez, A.J., Hundt, A.S., Hoonakker, R., Holden, R., and Gurses, A.P. (2014). Human Factors Systems Approach to Healthcare Quality and Patient Safety. *Applied Ergonomics*, 45(1), pp. 14–25. DOI: 10.1016/j.apergo.2013.04.023. 20, 26

Carroll, J.M., Kellogg, W.A., and Rosson, M.B. (1991). The Task–Artifact Cycle. In J.M. Carroll (ed.), *Designing Interaction: Psychology at the Human–Computer Interface* (pp. 74–102). Cambridge: Cambridge University Press. 6

Clot, Y. (2010). Clinique of activity: The Dialogue as Instrument. In A. Sannino, H. Daniels, and K.D. Gutiérrez (eds.), *Learning and Expanding with Activity Theory* (pp. 286–302). New York: Cambridge University Press. 41

Daniellou, F. (2005). The French-Speaking Ergonomists' Approach to Work Activity: Cross In-fluences of Field Intervention and Conceptual Models. *Theoretical Issues in Ergonomics Science*, 6(5), pp. 409–28. DOI: 10.1080/14639220500078252. 15

Daniellou, F. and Rabardel, P. (2005). Activity-Oriented Approaches to Ergonomics: Some Tra-ditions and Communities. *Theoretical Issues in Ergonomics Science*, 6(5), pp. 353-57. DOI: 10.1080/14639220500078351. 15

Dewey, J. (1999). *The Quest for Certainty: A Study of the Relation of Knowledge and Action* (in Finnish translation). Helsinki: Gaudeamus. 40

Dewey, J. (2002). *Human Nature and Conduct*. Toronto: Dover Publications, Inc. 22, 34, 62

Dul, J., Bruder, R., Buckle, P., Carayon, P., Falzon, P., Marras, W.S., Wilson, J.R., and van der Doelen, B. (2012). A Strategy for Human Factors/Ergonomics: Developing the Discipline and Profession. *Ergonomics*, 55(4), pp. 377–95. DOI: 10.1080/00140139.2012.661087. 9, 10

Engeström, Y. (1987). *Expansive Learning*. Jyväskylä, Finland: Orienta. 12, 21, 25, 26

Engeström, Y. (2007). Putting Vygotsky to Work: The Cange Laboratory as an Application of Double stimulation. In H. Daniels, M. Cole, and J.V. Wertsch (eds.), *The Cambridge Com-panion to Vygotsky* (pp. 363–82). Cambridge: Cambridge University Press. DOI: 10.1017/CCOL0521831040.015.

Engeström, Y. (2011). From Design Experiments to Formative Interventions. *Theory and Psychology*, 21(5), pp. 598–628. DOI: 10.1177/0959354311419252. 37, 42

Falzon, P. (2008). Enabling Safety: Issues in Design and Continuous Design. *Cognition, Technology and Work*, 10(1), pp. 7–14. DOI: 10.1007/s10111-007-0072-1. 43

Filippi, G. (2006). "Studying Computerized Emergency Operating Procedures to Evaluate the Impact of Strong Procedure Guidance on Operators' Work Practices." Paper presented at the *American Nuclear Society's 5th International Topical Meeting on Nuclear Plant In-strumentation, Controls, and Human Machine Interface Technology* (NPIC&HMIT 2006); Albuquerque, New Mexico. 50

Findeli, A. (2001). Rethinking Design Education for the 21st Century: Theoretical, Methodological and Ethical Discussion. *Design Issues*, 17(1), pp. 5–17. DOI: 10.1162/07479360152103796. 43

Flach, J., Mulder, M., and van Paassen, M. (2004). The Concept of Situation in Psychology. In S. Branbury and S. Tremblay (eds.), *A Cognitive Approach to Situation Awareness: Theory and Application*. pp. 42–60. Aldershot: Ashgate. 22, 30

Gibson, J.J. (1979). *The Ecological Approach to Visual Perception*. Boston: Houghton Mifflin. 17, 23

Grote, G. (2012). Safety Management in Different High-Risk Domains—All the Same? *Safety Science*, 50(10), pp. 1983–92. DOI: 10.1016/j.ssci.2011.07.017. 111

H2020 (2014). *Work Program 2014–2015: Future and Emerging Technologies* (C (2014)4995 of 22 July 2014). Brussels: European Commission. 112

Hollnagel, E. (2006). Resilience—the Challenge of the Unstable. In E. Hollnagel, D. Woods, and N. Leveson (eds.), *Resilience Engineering: Concepts and Precepts*. pp. 9–17). Aldershot: Ashgate. 8

Hollnagel, E. and Woods, D. (2005). *Joint Cognitive Systems: Foundations of Cognitive Systems Engineering*. Boca Raton, Florida: Taylor and Francis. DOI: 10.1201/9781420038194. 23

Hollnagel, E., Woods, D.D., and Leveson, N. (eds.) (2006). *Resilience Engineering: Concepts and Precepts*. Aldershot: Ashgate. 111

Hollnagel, E., Paries, J., Woods, D., and Wreathall, J. (eds.) (2011). *Resilience Engineering in Practice: A Guidebook*. Farnham: Ashgate.

Huang, F. and Hwang, S.-L. (2009). Experimental Studies of Computerized Procedures and Team Size in Nuclear Power Plant Operations. *Nuclear Engineering and Design*, 239(2), pp. 373–80. DOI: 10.1016/j.nucengdes.2008.10.009. 5

Ilyenkov, E. (1977). *Dialectical Logic: Essays on Its History and Theory*. Moscow: Progress. 40

Ingold, T. (2000). *The Perception of the Environment: Essays on Livelihood, Dwelling and Skill*. London: Routledge. DOI: 10.4324/9780203466025. 22, 27

ISO 11064 (2000). *Ergonomic Design of Control Centers* (parts 1, 2, and 3).

Järvilehto, T. (1994). *Man and His Environment: Essentials of Systemic Psychology* (in Finnish translation). Oulu, Finland: Pohjoinen. 22, 30

Järvilehto, T. (1998). The Theory of the Organism–Environment System (I): Description of the Theory. *Integrative Physiological and Behavioral Science*, 33(4), pp. 317–30. DOI: 10.1007/BF02688700. 17, 22

Joas, H. (1996). *The Creativity of Action*. Cambridge: Polity Press. 35

Kaarstad, M., Nystad, E., and Strand, S. (2011). Work Practices and Cooperation in a Near Future and Far Future Operational Environment. In A.B. Skjerve and A. Bye (eds.), *Simulator-Based Human Factors Studies across 25 Years*. London: Springer. 6

Kaptelinin, V. and Nardi, B. (2006). *Acting with Technology: Activity Theory and Interaction Design*. Cambridge, Massachusetts: The MIT Press. 26

Kaptelinin, V. and Nardi, B. (2012). *Activity Theory in HCI*, Vol. 13 in the series Synthesis Lectures on Human centered Informatics, edited by J.M. Carroll. Morgan & Claypool. DOI: 10.2200/S00413ED1V01Y201203HCI013. 26, 72

Keinonen, T. (2007). "Immediate, Product and Remote Design." Paper presented at the *International Association of Societies of Design and Research Conference*; Hong Kong. 44

Kleiner, B.M. (2006). Macroergonomics: Analysis and Design of Work Systems. *Applied Ergonomics*, 37(1), pp. 81–9. DOI: 10.1016/j.apergo.2005.07.006. 20, 26

Koski-Jännes, A. (1999). From Addiction to Self-Governance. In Y. Engeström, R. Miettinen, and R.-L. Punamäki (eds.), *Perspectives on Activity Theory*. Cambridge: Cambridge University Press. DOI: 10.1017/CBO9780511812774.028. 38

Kuutti, K. (2009). Artifacts, Activities, and Design Knowledge. In S. Poggenpohl and K. Sato (eds.), *Design Integrations: Research and Collaboration*. pp. 67–85. Chicago/Bristol: University of Chicago Press/Intellect Ltd. 43

Kuutti, K. and Bannon, L.J. (2014). "The Turn to Practice in HCI: Towards a Research Agenda." Paper presented at *CHI 2014*, One of a CHInd; Toronto. DOI: 10.1145/2556288.2557111. 9, 15

Laarni, J., Norros, L., and Salo, L. (2006). "Control Room Modernization at Finnish Nuclear Power Plants—Two Projects Compared." Paper presented at the *ANS International Topical Meeting on Nuclear Plant Instrumentation, Controls, and Human Machine Interface Technology*; Albuquerque, New Mexico. 5

Laarni, J., Norros, L., Savioja, P., and Rantanummmi, P. (2011). "Development of Training Programs for Nuclear Power Plant Personnel—Lessons Learned from Finnish Development Projects." Paper presented at the *Enlarged Halden Project Group Meeting*; Sandefjord, Norway. 9, 99

Laarni, J., Savioja, P., Norros, L., Liinasuo, M., Wahlström, M., and Salo, L. (2014). "Conducting Multistage HFE Validations—Constructing Systems Usability Case." Paper presented at the *International Symposium on Future I&C for Nuclear Power Plants/International Symposium on Symbiotic Nuclear Power 2014*; Jeju, Korea. 91

Laarni, J., Karvonen, H., Koskinen, H., Liinasuo, M., Norros, L., Savioja, P., Salo, L., Laakso, A.-M., and Lehtonen, M. (2013). "A Stepwise Validation Process for the Main Control Room of Fortum Loviisa Nuclear Power Plant." Paper presented at the *Enlarged Halden Project Group Meeting*; Storefjell, Norway. 91

Lawson, B. (1980). *How Designers Think*. London: The Architectural Press. 43

Leont'ev, A.N. (1978). *Activity, Consciousness, and Personality*. Englewood Cliffs, California: Prentice Hall. 11, 21, 25, 32

Leontjew, A.N. (1973). *Probleme der Entwicklung des Psychischen*. Berlin: Volk und Wissen. 32

Määttänen, P. (2009). *Toiminta ja Kokemus [Action and experience]*. Helsinki: Gaudeamus Helsinki University Press. 34, 35

MacIntyre, A. (1984). *After Virtue: Study in Moral Theory* (2nd ed.). Notre Dame, Indiana: University of Notre Dame Press. 28

Megill, A. (1997). Four senses of objectivity. In A. Megill (ed.), *Rethinking Objectivity*. Durham, North Carolina/London: Duke University Press. 41

Merleau-Ponty, M. (1986). *The Phenomenology of Perception*. London: Routledge and Kegan Paul. 17, 22

Miettinen, R. (2006). Epistemology of Transformative Material Activity: John Dewey's Pragmatism and Cultural Historical Activity Theory. *Journal of the Theory of Social Behavior*, 36(4), pp. 389–408. DOI: 10.1111/j.1468-5914.2006.00316.x. 41

MMOtion (2011). *Roadmap of R&D Needs for a Better Integration of Human and Organizational Factors in the Design and Operation of Nuclear Installations*. Brussels: Euratom. 70

Naikar, N. (2013). *Work Domain Analysis: Concepts, Guidelines, and Cases*. Boca Raton, Florida: Taylor and Francis. DOI: 10.1201/b14774. 30

Neisser, U. (1976). *Cognition and Reality*. San Francisco: W.H. Freeman.

Nicolini, D. (2013). *Practice Theory, Work, and Organization: An Introduction*. Oxford: Oxford University Press. 10, 16, 17, 18, 19, 21, 27

Norros, L. (2004). *Acting under Uncertainty: The Core-Task Analysis in Ecological Study of Work* (VTT publications 546). Espoo, Finland: VTT. Available also at http://www.vtt.fi/inf/pdf/publications/2004/P546.pdf. 18, 25, 27, 28, 30, 33, 34, 60, 63

Norros, L. (2014). Developing Human Factors/Ergonomics as a Design Discipline. *International Journal of Applied Ergonomics*, 45(1), 61–71. DOI:10.1016/j.apergo.2013.04.024. 10

Norros, L. and Nuutinen, M. (2002). The Core-Task Concept as a Tool to Analyze Working Practices. In N. Boreham, R. Samurçay, and M. Fischer (eds.), *Work Process Knowledge*. pp. 25–39. London: Routledge. 25

Norros, L. and Nuutinen, M. (2005). Performance-Based Usability Evaluation of a Safety Information and Alarm System. *International Journal of Human–Computer Studies*, 63(3), pp. 328–61. DOI: 10.1016/j.ijhcs.2005.03.004. 79

Norros, L. and Savioja, P. (2004). "Usability Evaluation of Complex Systems: A Literature Review." Helsinki: Radiation and Nuclear Safety Authority. 6, 100

Norros, L., Liinasuo, M., and Savioja, P. (2014). Operators' Orientations to Procedure Guidance in NPP Process Control. *Cognition, Technology and Work* (online). DOI:10.1007/s10111-014-0274-2. 97

Norros, L., Koskinen, H., Hildebrand, M., Paulus, V., and Gauthier, B. (2011). "Methodology for Evaluation of Innovative Concepts: Case FITNESS Control Station Concept." Paper presented at the Enlarged Halden Project Group Meeting; Sandefjord, Norway. 70, 71

NUREG-0700 (2002). "Human–System Interface Design Review Guidelines." 6

NUREG-0711 (2004). "Human Factors Engineering Program Review Model." Washington, DC: United States Nuclear Regulatory Commission. 9, 90, 100

O'Hara, J. and Persensky, J. (2011). Human Performance and Plant Safety Performance: Establishing a Technical Basis and Framework for Evaluating New Human–System Interfaces. In A.B. Skjerve and A. Bye (eds.), *Simulator-Based Human Factors Studies across 25 Years.* London: Springer. 6

O'Hara, J., Pirus, D., and Beltratcchi, L. (2003). *Information Display: Considerations for Designing Modern Computer-Based Display Systems.* Palo Alto, California: Electric Power Research Institute. 5, 70

ONR. (2014). "The Purpose, Scope, and Content of Safety Cases Rev. 3:" UK Office for Nuclear Regulation. 39

Papin, B. (2002). "Integration of Human Factors Requirements in the Design of Future Plants." Paper presented at the Enlarged Halden Program Group Meeting; Storefjell, Norway. 111

Paunonen, H. (1997). *Roles of Informating [sic] Process Control Systems* (Ph.D. thesis). Tampere, Finland: Tampere University of Technology. 6

Peirce, C.S. (1958). Letters to Lady Welby. In P. Wiener (ed.), *Selected Writings of C.C. Peirce.* pp. 380–432. New York: Dover Publications. 22, 34

Peirce, C.S. (1998a). The Harvard Lectures on Pragmatism. In *The Essential Peirce: Selected Philosophical Writings* (Vol. 2, pp. 133–241). Bloomington, Indiana / Indianapolis: Indiana University Press. 11

Peirce, C.S. (1998b). Pragmatism. In *The Essential Peirce: Selected Philosophical Writings* (Vol. 2, pp. 398–433). Bloomington, Indiana / Indianapolis: Indiana University Press. 34

Peirce, C.S. (1998c). Pragmatism as the logic of abduction. In *The Essential Peirce: Selected Philosophical Writings* (Vol. 2, pp. 226–41). Bloomington, Indiana/Indianapolis: Indiana University Press. 34

Peirce, C.S. (1998d). Sundry logical conceptions. In *The Essential Peirce: Selected Philosophical Writings*. pp. 267–88. Bloomington, Indiana/Indianapolis: Indiana University Press. 36

Peirce, C.S. (1998e). What is a sign? In *The Essential Peirce: Selected Philosophical Writings* (Vol. 2, pp. 4–11). Bloomington, Indiana/Indianapolis: Indiana University Press. 62

Petersen, J. (2004). Control situations in supervisory control. *Cognition, Technology and Work*, 6(4), pp. 266–74. DOI: 10.1007/s10111-004-0164-0. 30

Pettersen, K. A. (2013). Acknowledging the Role of Abductive Thinking: A Way out of Proceduralization for Safety Management and Oversight? In C. Bieder and M. Bourrier (Eds.), *Trapping Safety into Rules. How Desirable or Avoidable is Proceduralisation* (pp. 107-120). Farnham: Aschgate. 36

Pettersen, K.A., McDonald, N., and Engen, O.A. (2010). Rethinking the Role of Social Theory in Socio-Technical Analysis: A Critical Realist Approach to Aircraft Maintenance. *Cognition, Technology and Work*, 12(3), pp. 181–91. DOI: 10.1007/s10111-009-0133-8. 19

Pierce, J., Strengers, Y., Sengers, P., and Bødker, S. (2013). Introduction to the Special Issue on Practice-Oriented Approaches to Sustainable HCI. *ACM Transactions on Computer–Human Interaction* (TOCHI), 20(4), pp. 1–8. DOI: 10.1145/2509404.2494260. 21, 40, 44

Plant, K.L. and Stanton, N.A. (2013). The Explanatory Power of Schema Theory: Theoretical Foundations and Future Application in Ergonomics. *Ergonomics*, 56(1), pp. 1–15. DOI: 10.1080/00140139.2012.736542. 37

Rabardel, P. and Béguin, P. (2005). Instrument Mediated Activity: From Subject Development to Anthropometric Design. *Theoretical Issues in Ergonomics Science*, 6(5), pp. 429–61. DOI: 10.1080/14639220500078179. 37

Rabardel, P. and Duvenci-Langa, S. (2002). Technological Change and the Construction of Competence. In N. Boreham, R. Samurçay, and M. Fischer (eds.), *Work Process Knowledge*. pp. 55–73. London: Routledge. 28

Rasmussen, J. (1986). *Information Processing and Human–Machine Interaction*. Amsterdam: North-Holland. 11, 30, 57

Roth, E. and O'Hara, J. (2002). "Integrating Digital and Conventional Human–System Interfaces: Lessons Learned from a Control Room Modernization Program." Washington, DC: Nuclear Regulatory Commission. 5

Rückriem, G. (2009). Digital Technology and Mediation: A Challenge to Activity Theory. In A. Sannino, H. Daniels, and K.D. Gutiérrez (eds.), *Learning and Expanding with Activity Theory.* pp. 88–111. New York: Cambridge University Press. DOI: 10.1017/CBO9780511809989.007. 37

Salo, L. and Savioja, P. (2014). "Development of a HFE Program for an Operating NPP: Balancing between Existing Design Practices and Fuman Factors Standards." Paper presented at the International Symposium on Future I&C for Nuclear Power Plants/International Symposium on Symbiotic Nuclear Power; Jeju, Korea. 100, 103, 104

Sannino, A., Daniels, H., and Gutiérrez, K.D. (eds.) (2009). *Learning and Expanding with Activity Theory.* New York: Cambridge University Press. DOI: 10.1017/CBO9780511809989. 21, 109

Savioja, P. (2014). Evaluating Systems Usability in Complex Work: Development of a Systemic Usability Concept to Benefit Control Room Design (Ph.D. thesis). Finland: Aalto University, School of Science. Available at http://www.vtt.fi/inf/pdf/science/2014/S57.pdf (VTT Science 57). 30, 43, 74

Savioja, P. and Norros, L. (2008). Systems Usability—Promoting Core-Task Oriented Work Practices. In E. Law, E.T. Hvannberg, and G. Cockton (eds.), *Maturing Usability: Quality in Software, Interaction and Value.* pp. 123–43. London: Springer. 37

Savioja, P. and Norros, L. (2012). Systems Usability Framework for Evaluating Tools in Safety-Critical work. *Cognition, Technology and Work,* 15(3), pp. 1–21. DOI: 10.1007/s10111-012-0224-9. 30, 37, 38, 39

Savioja, P., Norros, L., and Salo, L. (2012a). "Functional Situation Models in Analyzes of Operating Practices in Complex Qork." Paper presented at the European Conference on Cognitive Ergonomics; Edinburgh, Scotland. DOI: 10.1145/2448136.2448148. 30, 32

Savioja, P., Norros, L., Liinasuo, M., and Laarni, J. (2011). "Human Factors Engineering—Current Practices and Development Needs in Finland." Paper presented at ICI2011 (the *International Symposium on Future I&C for Nuclear Power Plants + Cognitive Systems Engineering in Process Control + International Symposium on Symbiotic Nuclear Power 2011*); Daejeon, Korea. 100

Savioja, P., Norros, L., Salo, L., and Aaltonen, I. (2014). Identifying Resilience in ProceduraliZed Accident Management Activity of NPP Operating Crews. *Safety Science,* 68(October), pp. 258–274. DOI: 10.1016/j.ssci.2014.04.008. 50

Savioja, P., Aaltonen, I., Karvonen, H., Koskinen, H., Laarni, J., Liinasuo, M., Norros, L., and Salo, L. (2012b). "Systems Usability Concerns in Hybrid Control Rooms." Paper presented at the *8th International Topical Meeting on Nuclear Plant Instrumentation, Control, and Human Machine Interface Technology*, San Diego, California. 6

Schatzki, T. R. (2005). Peripheral Vision. *The Sites of Organizations Organization Studies*, 26 (3), 465-484. DOI: 10.1177/0170840605050876. 17

Schatzki, T.R., Knorr-Cetina, K., and Savigny, E.V. (eds.) (2001). *The Practice Turn in Contemporary Theory*. London/New York: Routledge. 17

Skjerve, A.-B. and Bye, A. (eds.) (2011). *Simulator-Based Human-Factors Studies across 25 Years*. London: Springer. DOI: 10.1007/978-0-85729-003-8. 5

Skraaning Jr., G., Lau, N., Welch, R., Nihlwing, C., Andresen, G., Brevig, L. H., Veland, O., Jamieson,G., Burns,C., and Kwok, G. (2007). *The Ecological Interface Design Experiment* (2005). Halden, Norway: OECD Halden Reactor Project. 5

Stanton, N.A. (2006). Hierarchical Task Analysis: Developments, Applications, and Extensions. *Applied Ergonomics*, 37(1), pp. 55–79. DOI: 10.1016/j.apergo.2005.06.003. 57

Tommila, T., Valkonen, J., Raatikainen, M., and Uusitalo, E. (2013). Safety Requirements Specification and Management in Nuclear Power Plants. In K. Simola (ed.). *Interim Report of SAFIR2014, the Finnish Research Program on Nuclear Power Plant Safety 2011–2014* (VTT Technology, Vol. 80, pp. 74–83). Espoo, Finland: VTT Technical Research Center of Finland. 112

Vicente, K.J. (1999). *Cognitive Work Analysis: Toward Safe, Productive, and Healthy Computer based Work*. Mahwah, New Jersey: Lawrence Erlbaum Publishers. 11, 12, 27, 28, 30, 57, 60

von Uexküll, J. and Kriszat, G. (1932). *Streifzüge durch die Umwelten von Tieren und Menschen*. Frankfurt am Main, Germany: Fischer. 17

Vygotsky, L.S. (1978). *Mind in Society: The Development of Higher Psychological Processes*. Cambridge, Massachusetts: Harvard University Press. 11, 21, 37, 42

Wahlström, M., Karvonen, H., Kaasinen, E., and Mannonen, P. (accepted for publication). Designing for Future Professional Activity—Examples from Ship-Bridge Concept Design. *Ergonomics and Usability in Design*. 29

Walker, G., Stanton, N., Salmon, P., and Jenkins, D. (2007). A Review of Sociotechnical Systems Theory: A Classic Concept for New Command and Control Paradigms. Internet: Human Factors Integration Defence Technology Center. 20

Wartofsky, M. (1979). *Models: Representations and Scientific Understanding*. Dordrecht, Netherlands: Reidel. DOI: 10.1007/978-94-009-9357-0. 40

Weick, K.E. and Sutcliffe, K.M. (2007). *Managing the Unexpected: Resilient Performance in an Age of Uncertainty*. San Francisco: Jossey-Bass. 36

Wilson, J. (2014). Fundamentals of Systems Ergonomics/Human Factors. *Applied Ergonomics*, 45(1), pp. 5–13. DOI: 10.1016/j.apergo.2013.03.021. 20, 26

Wilson, J. and Carayon, P. (2014). Special Issue: Systems Ergonomics/Human Factors. *Applied Ergonomics*, 45(1), pp. 1–132. 9

Woods, D. (1988). Coping with Complexity: The Psychology of Human Behavior in Complex Systems. In L.P. Goodstein, H.B. Andersen, and S.E. Olsen (eds.), *Tasks, Errors, and Mental Models: A Festschrift to Celebrate the 60th Birthday of Professor Jens Rasmussen* (pp. 128–48). London: Taylor and Francis. 27

Woods, D. and Hollnagel, E. (2006). *Joint Cognitive Systems—Patterns in Cognitive Systems Engineering*. Boca Raton, Florida: Taylor and Francis. DOI: 10.1201/9781420005684. 23

Wright, P. and McCarthy, J. (2010). *Experience-Centered Design: Designers, Users, and Communities in Dialogue*. Lexington, Kentucky: Morgan & Claypool Publishers. DOI: 10.2200/S00229ED1V01Y201003HCI009. 38, 44

Wulf, V., Rohde, M., Pipek, V., and Stevens, G. (2011). "Engaging with Practices: Design Case Studies as a Research Framework in CSC." Paper presented at the *ACM 2011 Conference on Computer-supported Cooperative Work*; Hangzhou, China. 44

Yang, C.W., Yenn, T., and Lin, C.J. (2010). Assessing Team Workload under Automation Based on a Subjective Performance Measure. *Safety Science*, 48(7), pp. 914–20. DOI: 10.1016/j.ssci.2010.03.011. 6

Zink, K.J. (2014). Designing Sustainable Work Systems: The Need for a Systems Approach. *Applied Ergonomics*, 45(1), pp. 126–32. DOI: 10.1016/j.apergo.2013.03.023. 20

Author Biographies

Leena Norros

Research Professor (emerita) Leena Norros is an industrial psychologist working on human factors of complex industrial systems. She received Dr.rer.nat. at the Technical University of Dresden, Germany, and Ph.D. in psychology at the University of Helsinki, Finland. She created a human factors research team at the VTT Technical Research Centre of Finland and spent most of her career leading the team. Her main interest is the understanding of work activity in real-life contexts, for which she has created new concepts and methods. She acts as docent at Helsinki University and lectures on human factors at the University of Helsinki and Aalto University. She has published widely and participates actively in international forums of human factors/ergonomics.

Paula Savioja

Paula Savioja works as a Research Team Leader at VTT Technical Research Centre of Finland. She received her master's degree from Helsinki University of Technology from the department of Automation and Systems Technology. She completed her doctoral studies at Aalto University School of Science with a dissertation labeled "Evaluating Systems Usability in Complex Work." Savioja has worked over ten years at VTT in different research and development projects in various safety critical domains. Her expertise is human factors approach to design and development of complex socio-technical systems.

Hanna Koskinen

Hanna Koskinen is a Research Scientist at VTT Technical Research Centre of Finland. Her research focuses on human factors in complex systems and in particular design and development of tools for professional use in safety critical work. She holds a Master of Arts in Industrial Design from University of Lapland with a minor in work psychology and management from Helsinki University of Technology.

Printed in the United States
by Baker & Taylor Publisher Services